P9-ARS-599

The Government of
FRANCE

E. Drexel Godfrey, Jr.

CROWELL COMPARATIVE GOVERNMENT SERIES

Thomas Y. Crowell Company
NEW YORK ESTABLISHED 1834

INTRODUCTION

This booklet is an introduction to French government and politics, part of a series organized as a comparative study of world governments today. It sketches the historical background of the French nation and people and then proceeds to an analysis of formal institutions and the functions of government in all areas.

The risks of writing on the French scene are well known to all professionals in the field. Even as this volume was being prepared for the printer, reasonable men might have doubted that its subject, de Gaulle's Republic, would survive through the processes of printing, binding, and distribution. The author found that it was difficult, even in the face of this possibility, to separate man from institution, not to include the imposing figure of the General on almost every page. Nevertheless, he is hopeful that some of the seemingly ineradicable elements of French political life, which even the Fifth Republic is likely to leave unchanged, come clear. He is equally hopeful that the uniqueness—and hence possibly the brittleness—of the Fifth Republic's political mores have been sufficiently exposed to offer a reader living perhaps in the presence of the Sixth Republic an interesting historical commentary.

My thanks for help in the preparation of this volume must first go to my readers, principally Edgar Furniss of Princeton University and Val Lorwin of the University of Oregon. They must share the credit for whatever merits are to be found in these pages; the author is entirely responsible, however, for opinions expressed, facts presented, and interpretations attempted. My thanks also go to my typists, especially Mrs. Dorothy James of Kalamazoo, Michigan, and Miss Mary Dolores LePore of Washington, D.C., and to Drex, Dan, and Peter, whose interest in the project never failed.

E. D. G., Jr.

Alexandria, Virginia
June, 1961

 Manufactured in the United States of America by The Colonial Press Inc. Library of Congress Catalog Card Number: 61-15525. Series design by Joan Wall.

EDITOR'S FOREWORD

In our time the study of comparative government constitutes one of many fields or specialities in political science. But it is worth recalling that the most distinguished political scientists of the ancient world would have had difficulty recognizing the present-day distinction between the study of comparative government and study in other subject areas of the discipline. Think of Plato, for example, whose works abound in references to the political systems of his own and earlier days. Or consider Aristotle, whose *Politics* and related writings were based on an examination of more than one hundred constitutions. Twenty centuries after Aristotle the comparative emphasis continued strong in the work of Montesquieu and Rousseau, among others. In the nineteenth century the comparative tradition entered upon a period of decline, but there are signs that the merits of comparative political analysis are once more gaining recognition. At many colleges and universities, the introductory course in political science is no longer focused exclusively on American government. The comparative approach—in politics, in law, in administration—is becoming increasingly important in the political science curriculum.

This booklet, one of a series, is designed to reflect that approach, without, however, marking a sharp departure from the substance and method of most comparative government courses. With one exception (Arnold J. Heidenheimer, *The Government of Germany: West and East*), each booklet deals with one national government, but the booklets are distinctively comparative in at least two senses. Most of them include material descriptive of other political systems, especially that of the United States. In addition, the booklets follow a common outline, so far as possible, and are designed to promote comparative treatment. Of course, there is nothing to keep the instructor or student from treating a particular governmental system in isolation, if he chooses to do so. On the other hand, his approach to political institutions and functions can be as comparative as he wishes.

A further advantage of this series is that each booklet has been written by a distinguished scholar and authority in the field; each author is personally and professionally familiar with the political system he treats. Finally, the separate booklets make it possible for the instructor to design his course in accordance with his own interest or the interests of his students. One booklet may be substituted for another or any booklet put aside for one semester without affecting the others. The booklets, in short, unlike most one-volume textbooks, give the instructor maximum freedom in organizing his course. This freedom will be virtually unlimited as the forthcoming titles in this series complete a survey of representative governments of the world.

But to return to Aristotle once again, it remains true that the best judges of the feast are not the cooks but the guests. I have tried to indicate why, in my view, the recipe for the series is a good one. Let all those who teach comparative government, and all those who take courses in that field, proceed to judge the booklets for themselves.

ARNOLD A. ROGOW

CONTENTS

1 - The French Republican Tradition

Introduction

A perceptive son of France once remarked that throughout history his motherland had been obliged to live dangerously. This observer saw France's perilous history as the consequence of her exposed geographic position. Others have claimed that the French people lived dangerously because their Celtic origins compelled them to combativeness; still others have ascribed France's adventurous life history to an enquiring and even aspiring national mentality, which some Frenchmen turned to individual genius in art, literature and philosophy, while others were building both the most brilliant and the most sordid of political traditions. Whatever the true causes, we are here concerned with a people whose relationship to life is as dramatic as their history has been, a people who have employed the same sense of daring in choosing their art forms, their fashions, and their cuisine, as they have in building three empires, in experimenting with almost every known form of political system, and in fighting innumerable wars and revolutions. It is no paradox then that the Frenchman can even carry his disdain for the norms of life, his apathy toward the world around him to a point of trembling danger.

France has often been described as a woman. The French people themselves have frequently chosen feminine figures to symbolize their country, suggesting in so doing the infinite variety they find in their homeland and the range of emotions which it induces in them. Indeed the Frenchman sees in France all the qualities of femininity—the softness of her countryside, the passion of her people, the pettiness of her national jealousies, the capacity to endure suffering under indignities, even the splendid ugliness of her older cities. They may love or scorn France, but because she is a woman they cannot ignore her. In fact the absorption of the French people with France is the hallmark of their political life.

When a Frenchman speaks passionately of France he may be identifying himself with a moment in her history of which he particularly approves (or abhors), or he may be expressing admiration (or despair) of the whole kaleidescope of French history, accomplishments, and failures. In his mind the motherland has not only lived dangerously but vividly; it has produced heroes and villains, but however he regards them they are extraordinary. There is on the one hand Napoleon and on the other Laval; or, off the political stage, Molière, Voltaire, Matisse, and Anouilh. His newspapers are primarily political (although this aspect of French life seems to be changing). They may be venal, they may be inaccurate, they may be in the pay of the government, and sometimes even in the pay of a foreign government, but they are unabashedly political and they are most often selected by the subway reader according to their political character. In a sense, the Frenchman seeks to share the excitement of great political ideas or stirring moments of political upheaval and change in which he—or his ancestors—have taken part. This does not mean, necessarily, that he relates himself to a specific or single current of political thought—a French Communist can and does delight in Louis XIV's Palace of Versailles—but it does mean that as a Frenchman he derives considerable satisfaction from sharing in the variety and richness of France's history. Today it is the mode in France to scoff at politics; many Frenchmen avoid identifying themselves politically in any way; they proclaim proudly that they are not *engagés,* involved in the political storms of the moment. But even those who wear their indifference proudly can point to an illustrious tradition of "non-engagement" which has preceded their generation.

Perhaps the cause for the Frenchman's fascination with the game of politics—even though he may be unwilling to cheer any of the players—is that French political history is a continuous current. There are almost no extinct species in French political zoology. Most of the present-day parties in France claim multiple connections with the past. The Socialists, for example, claim the Jacobins of 1792, the Communards of 1870, and the Second International of Marx and Lenin as their forebears. It is significant that as recently as the crisis of January, 1960, serious political commentators were speculating whether, if President de Gaulle were deposed, a dark horse compromise candidate for the assumption of his powers might not be found in the Count of Paris, the pretender to the long defunct French throne! Thus, political traditions and the attitudes or beliefs associated with them rarely die in France, although they may be adapted to existing conditions. They may disappear for long periods, but somewhere they are being cherished to re-emerge when conditions are again favorable. Even French fascism, which certainly seemed to have been obliterated by the national revulsion against the collaborators during and after the German occupation of France in World War II, appears now to have taken new root in Algeria, where several admittedly neo-fascist movements flourish.

For the most part, however, French political movements, although they may cling to the importance of their origins and to a few fundamental points of doctrine, go through a process of evolution as society changes around them, or as their electorate shifts away from them or, in some cases, as the goals which they originally set for themselves are attained. The most celebrated example of this is the Radical-Socialist Party which began life in the 1870s to preserve political and civil liberties and lay republicanism when neither was secure in France. The now sadly splintered party retains only the name from its past; far from being radical or socialist, it is rather stuffily conservative, fashions its position on issues according to its electoral prospects, and only occasionally can come to agreement within itself on a firm matter of principle.

The Historical Perspective of French Politics

French political history can be seen as a maze of threads beginning in various places, frequently crossing and tangling with one another, with new strands entering from time to time. To unravel this jumble for an understanding of its separate parts one must begin with the great rent in French history—the Revolution of 1789. The French, with great drama, brilliant political skill, and eventually with a missionary and military zeal which threatened *anciens régimes* throughout much of the rest of Europe, routed the monarchy, the aristocracy, and the privileged Roman Catholic Church in the name of liberty, equality, and the republican form of government. The old order was defeated but the nineteenth century, and to delay for decades any definitive not destroyed. Its defenders were able to revive the monarchy in regulation of the Church's powers. Far more significant, however, was the creation of a hard core of anti-republicans, who would attempt to undermine all republics from First (1792) to Fifth (1958), and which even today is little reconciled to the processes of popular sovereignty.

The defenders of the revolution and the republic were not long in dividing over whether they would give priority to equality or to liberty. In the early revolutionary period a great effort was made to destroy the unequal political privileges of the titled and aristocratic classes. In keeping with the notion that despotism and oppression were primarily products of the heavy hand of the state, the elimination of privilege was at first undertaken with a minimum use of government machinery, and attempts were made to portray the results as the product of the direct voice of the people manifested through popular meetings. The Declaration of the Rights of Man, adopted tumultuously in the Revolutionary Assemblies, detailed the expectations of humble Frenchmen to be treated with equal justice before the law, and to be regarded as equivalent to all other Frenchmen in the exercise of their rights and in the day-to-day conduct of their lives. The "Rights of Man" was primarily a political document; it represented the momentary ascendancy of the libertarians over the egalitarians; it disregarded the possibility that the economic advantages of a few could, even in a democratic republic, distort the political liberties of the majority.

There were, however, strong undercurrents in the revolution which were bent on a leveling of all economic and social distinctions between men. The top-heavy and aggressively power-hungry dictatorship of the Jacobins at the close of the revolutionary period was a move toward the use of the state as an instrument of vigorous social change. The efforts of the Jacobins did not prevail, and in fact were brutally snuffed out in the Napoleonic period which capped the revolution. However, the Jacobins added a new and powerful political strain to the matrix of French political development which was to assert itself several times in the nineteenth century, and most dynamically in the twentieth century.

In the nineteenth century the libertarians had only a shaky hold on France. This was a period of adaptation and experiment, as political strands became snarled by borrowing ideas from one another. The anti-revolutionists returned twice: first in the form of the brief reappearance of the legitimate monarchy of Louis XVIII in 1814, which was traditionalist in most respects, except that even the king acknowledged the existence of the "Rights of Man." The last curtain call of the legitimists was the puzzling, hybrid, liberal monarchy of Louis Philippe in 1830, which bowed to the traditionalists in its concept of monarchical sovereign authority, and to the liberals in its indulgence of parliamentary machinery for the exercise of power. At the outset the liberal monarchy paid lip service to the need for safeguarding the individual liberties of all citizens; the liberals quickly asserted that this protection was to guard their interests against encroachments by the king. Their claim was never recognized by the monarch, and in fact no resolution of this fundamental issue involving the nature of sovereign power was ever achieved. Finally, the revolution of 1848 put an end to the "liberal monarchy."

The most curious intermixture of political strands flowing from the Revolution was the imperial tradition—into which Napoleon Bonaparte stumbled, which his nephew perfected in the Second Empire—and which some modern pundits insist is experiencing a reincarnation in the Fifth Republic of General de Gaulle. The Napoleons cleverly exploited Rousseau's theory of the "general will," which in earlier days had exhilarated the flamboyant revolutionary assemblies. Their apologists insisted that the emperors' mandates to speak and act for France (unfettered by any intermediate body) were legitimate because they served the popular will. To ratify imperial decisions both Napoleons resorted to the use of popular referendums. According to their court theorists the popular will was thereby expressed in the imperial person. Like the Jacobins, the Bonapartes appealed to the masses not only for political approval, but for patriotic support. The Jacobin "nation in arms" became the Napoleonic conscript armies. In fact, however, the imperial tradition was, despite some trappings borrowed from the ferment of the revolution, counter-revolutionary and anti-republican. The first Napoleon liberally distributed thrones and titles to his family and friends. The apparatus of the state Napoleon I devised became a large, positive and arbitrary instrument, which operated as a force of its own, deriving its powers from his personal strength and the military might of the nation—not from the French people as such.

This typically French division between the organ of political will—the emperor—and the organs of state authority—the administration, the military establishment, the judiciary—represented a significant reorganization of the confusing, overlapping, and patchwork institutions that had sprung up unsystematically from the clamor of political beliefs and philosophies that had swept across France since the revolution. The distinction between government and administration, never very clear until then, was established in part by accident, in part through the vigorous action of Napoleon I, who simply presented France the organized bureaucratic institutions, codes of law, and systems of administrative regulation devised by his draftsmen, without justifying their birth in a new political synthesis. Not only is much of the state machinery created by Napoleon I still with France, but much of it remains still outside of the political arena. Since the last imperial epoch ended in 1870, many political battles have been fought, but they have largely been fought over governments and their policies, not over the administrative instruments of the governments in question. However, even today there are exceptions to this rule—as in the case of the political indiscretions of the armed forces in 1958, 1960, and 1961—and when these exceptions occur they are likely to prove the most trying and dangerous of all political difficulties for the French people. The Fifth Republic was born out of one of these exceptions; it is at this writing by no means firmly fixed, because of the circumstances surrounding its birth, which ran counter to what Frenchmen regard as the spirit of the republican tradition.

The hardiest political tradition spawned in the Revolution was the republican. In a sense it was the truest revolutionary element; it survived all manner of assaults, distortions, and even the bitter mockery of those who from time to time have momentarily eliminated it from the French political scene. As we have already noted, the revolutionaries who rose against the *ancien régime* tended to divide between those who sought political liberty and those who championed equality—although, of course, some pursued both goals. As the nineteenth century wore on and various political forms were tested, it was the libertarians who gave meaningful definition to republicanism, but more and more the image of the republic was employed by the egalitarians as a necessary beginning for the implantation of their own concepts of society.

The republicanism that emerged during the nineteenth century ultimately comprised only a few simple elements: insistence on the expression of the public will through a sovereign, directly elected assembly, a lay society, and distrust of executive authority as a threat to freedom, against which the people had an obligation to rise, when and if tyranny appeared imminent. Several times in both the nineteenth and twentieth century the people did in fact take to the barricades in defense of the republic against one of its own servants, usually a president or a premier flaunting the wishes of certain elements in the assembly. Of course, this particular form of civic violence could be easily justified by equating it with the most sacred of revolutionary traditions—the courageous revolt of the people against the soldiers of the tyrant king, his armies, and his tax collectors.

The egalitarians, at first Socialists and later Communists, have always employed the mystique of the barricades to their own advantage. In so doing they have associated their own goals with the strength and the emotional convictions of a much wider share of the French people than would have ever flocked to their banners alone. Thus, the revolution of 1848, ostensibly fought to restore republican government, resulted in the temporary establishment of a semi-socialist society. The Paris Commune that seized power in the capital city following the collapse of the Second Empire included various early pioneers of socialism, communism and anarchism, as well as some republicans. It was in turn smashed by other republicans, momentarily allied with counter-revolutionaries, who either regretted the passage of the empire or wished to take the occasion to bring back a diluted form of monarchy. When the rival claimants to monarchical power could not agree among themselves, the republicans triumphed by default. The Third Republic, begrudgingly put together by a constituent assembly in which a majority of the delegates were anti-republican, lived until 1940. It was finally destroyed by German arms after corrosive action by small pockets of anti-republicans and Communists had weakened in key places a political structure that had proved increasingly incapable of resolving modern problems.

Modern French political history spans the Third, Fourth, and Fifth Republics, interrupted between 1940 and 1944 by the Corporate State of Marshal Pétain, whose authority derived from German victory over France and not, by even the most generous interpretation, from the will of the French people. In many ways, the Vichy regime of Marshal Pétain symbolized all that was anti-republican in French life, while the *Résistance,* which fought it incessantly, has often been described as a pure revival of the republican spirit. Pétain and the ragtail crowd of fascists, anti-semites, disgruntled military officers, and crass opportunists who surrounded him set about to destroy all vestiges of republican democracy. Political authority was vested completely in the person of the Marshal; he was unencumbered by parliamentary organs, although a "corporate council" was ultimately established in which the interests of vocational and social groups were theoretically to be represented. In practice, employers represented labor, estate owners, the peasantry, etc. Most telling was the motto adopted by the new state. "Work, Family, and Fatherland" replaced "Liberty, Equality, and Fraternity." The traditionalist, conservative values of the *ancien régime* were reimposed by fiat on a scornful people who, except for a small minority, never accepted the fumbling and posturing of a regime that retained power at the point of German bayonets.

The *Résistance* that began organizing about a year after the French defeat contained elements from all shades of French republicanism, ranging from conservative nationalists who despised the ignominy of German occupation and the pandering of the Pétainists, to tough Communist leaders who had long since been forced underground. Several distinct *Résistance* networks existed in metropolitan France; many retained particular political colorations, others were heterogeneous. As Allied victory became imminent the *Résistance* organizations expanded operations, and adopted military as well as political characteristics. Eventually they came to dominate much of French life; in many sectors of the country *Résistance* elements were in control well before the arrival of Allied troops. When liberation was finally achieved the *Résistance* was a mighty force to be reckoned with. It had restored some of the Frenchman's self respect. No wonder then, that the new constitution which emerged from the ruins of postwar France was a reaffirmation of republican verities with strong leftist overtones adapted from the teachings of underground *maquisards.*

However, the strength of the Left was not sufficient to overcome some of the most awkward historical legacies of French political institutions. In fact the Fourth Republic was in many ways a streamlined version of the Third, emphasizing the purest republican traditions of a powerful, sovereign, popular Assembly, a weak executive, and an administrative apparatus that floated in an ambiguous limbo. Largely divorced from responsibility, the bureaucratic administration nevertheless had permanency and often greater power in an increasingly technological society than the incumbent premier. Yet the premiers and their cabinets soon became the targets for widespread criticism by the French public. Criticism finally turned to disgust, and when it did the Fourth Republic was replaced, virtually without regret, by the Fifth.

De Gaulle's new government—the subject of this book—is much more than just another step in French political history. In a certain sense it is a part of all them. It borrows threads from innumerable political strands; it is limited by other traditions that, although not concretely represented in the new regime, guide and channel the political attitudes and reflexes of the living Frenchmen who are its leaders. Conceived in adventure, the Fifth Republic is in the best tradition of French political history. It has already fashioned a *mystique* of its own, which will, if the lessons of the past are meaningful, outlast the Fifth Republic itself, and become embedded in the continuous flow of French political life.

2 - The Background of the Social Order

The People

Who are these people, then, who distill their political traditions from the sweat of revolutions, to whom a political philosophy is a way of life—not simply a descriptive program of the "ins" or of the "outs"? While Frenchmen dip luxuriously into a past of dramatic personal sacrifices, political courage, and the constant introduction of new philosophies and dynamic movements, why have they collectively become known in the second half of the twentieth century as a cynical, apathetic, and jaded citizenry? Why, until the coming of de Gaulle was France known as the sick man of Europe—a label originally applied to the crumbling Ottoman Empire at the eve of World War I?

There are, of course, no wholly satisfactory answers to the "why" of a people unless one consults the social anthropologists. But even this is difficult in France—there are many "French people": the hardy Savoyard of the mountains would no more fit the patterns of a study designed to describe the behavior, motivations, and mores of the Picards than would the urban, sophisticated Parisian.

There are some 45,000,000 Frenchmen in metropolitan

France and perhaps another million living away from the homeland who have transplanted their culture to their new outposts and still cling to French citizenship. Most French anthropologists claim, without much conviction, that the French people derive from Celtic tribes that came under Roman subjugation and influence some 2,000 years ago. Since that time the population has remained remarkably homogeneous, although there have been infusions of Spaniards in the west and south and there are large pockets of Italian and Polish *immigrés* in the northeast, and about 500,000 unassimilated Moslems from North Africa. Thus the sharp distinctions between Frenchmen from various corners of France, most marked in such things as language and family customs, are probably not due to ethnic differences as much as to the geographic, and until recent years the political, semi-isolation of the principal regions of the nation.

The modern French population is by world standards old. From the turn of the century until World War II the population declined absolutely; France had for the first four decades of the twentieth century the lowest birth rate in the world at a time when high medical standards were constantly extending the life span of the average Frenchman. In recent years, however, the population trend has been sharply changed. Under the stimulus of social welfare bonuses for large families and a clear reduction in the fear of recurrent unemployment, Frenchmen have once again started to reproduce themselves in large numbers. Over the next quarter century, at least, France seems destined to be a land topheavy at both ends of its population scale—more children and old people than productive adults—with all the familiar social obligations and responsibilities this imposes on a society.

We cannot hope to make an exhaustive analysis of the French personality—or better, the French personalities. However, some light may perhaps be shed on this complex subject by discussing certain influences which appear to affect great numbers of Frenchmen, regardless of age, regardless of the region they come from. These are, in other words, national influences which permeate France, although, of course, they may be more or less successfully resisted depending on the personality structure of each individual Frenchman, his life experience, local conditions, etc. Clearly, in some areas that are isolated, or even geographically separated from metropolitan France—such as Corsica and Algeria—these influences may be far less important to the citizen than local characteristics, traditions, and peculiarities.

Education

Because education is controlled by the national government in France right down to the form of the last third grade copy-book, the basic literary equipment of most Frenchmen is similar. Although some variation is permitted in the higher grade levels and between Catholic and national schools, the works of a few select writers are almost certain to find their way onto the desks of the vast majority of French children. There is heavy emphasis on philosophy: Voltaire, Rousseau, de Tocqueville, writers who carry forward into the present the three themes on which French educational indoctrination is based: rational reason, republican liberties and nationalism.

Voltaire, the eloquent spokesman of the pre-revolutionary period, the Enlightenment, waged subtle war against the institutions of the church and the state, which not only, as he said, robbed men of their liberty and reason, but obliterated the latter in the expectation thereby of reducing the number of competitors for power and for the satisfactions of society. In a time when the close alliance between princes of the church and princes of the realm produced a convenient and all-powerful oligarchy that brooked no dissent, no criticism, and regarded general public education as the work of Satan, these were bold and radical ideas. Voltaire viewed the dogmatism and despotism of the *ancien régime* as the most formidable barriers to truth, freedom and progress. In the pattern of his day, however, he was content to urge his enlightened philosophy on the leaders themselves, in the hopes that they would break the chains confining their own minds and build a new, more orderly, and just society. From him comes the open mind, the persistent inquisitiveness, the rejection of authority for its own sake so characteristic of the Frenchman. From Voltaire, and from the philosopher Descartes, too, springs the French habit of logical, rational inquiry, which often seems to the outsider to be an end in itself, a substitute for decisiveness and vigor. At its best this tendency is a constructive and maturing force for any people; at its worst it can lead to sterile cynicism and inaction. In France, of course, it does both.

Voltaire was primarily a liberator of men's minds—not of their persons. A reading of Voltaire may produce scepticism and even a certain self-satisfaction, but it will move few men to action. This stimulus can be found in the works of Rousseau, to which most French children are sooner or later exposed. Rousseau's *Social Contract* is based on the not entirely reasonable assumption that at bottom all men are good. Rousseau insisted on education for all—a revolutionary concept in its day—with the aim of equipping society's company of good men to rule themselves. Under these conditions a people could, he believed, be trusted to govern through majority rule; that is, the expression of the majority's wishes would happily coincide with what Rousseau called the "general will," or that which was in fact most desirable for the society. Even the school child readily sees the looseness of this philosophical construction, but the incompleteness of the thought pales before the enthusiastic tone of Rousseau's writings —their tumbling, racing course toward joy, toward the good life under government by the people. In his way Rousseau is for the Frenchman an antidote to the scepticism of Voltaire. Into the deep well of a Frenchman's heart he casts a stone or two—the belief in the goodness of man and the beautiful simplicity of rule by the majority—which for many Frenchmen become immutable principles.

Other writers, too—although they are not necessarily listed on the syllabi of the state schools—have been hungrily devoured by generations of French youth, and reflected in their subsequent behavior as political adults. Two, whose lives straddled the nineteenth and twentieth centuries, are supremely important. Alain (Émile A. Chartier), poet and philosopher, embodied the purest of libertarian individualism. He preached an unflagging personal resistance to authority in all its forms. No anarchist himself—he believed that an ideal form for the regulation of society probably was attainable—Alain's writings nevertheless stirred countless thousands to drift into a negative attitude toward government, authority, and the laws of the society. He found the greatest personal virtue in suspicion and defiance of tyranny. In the absence of an ideal society, however, his readers often used his teachings to justify their insistence on personal exemption from public responsibility.

Very different was the impact of essayist Charles Péguy, who for decades held court in a small bookstore near the Sorbonne, the great university of Paris. Péguy's writings were few, but over the years he established himself as the essence of humanitarianism. He appealed in his articles and lectures to the individual consciences of the French. The republican principles of social justice, human dignity, and equality could, he insisted, only be firmly established and preserved by their incarnation in the hearts of the citizenry. Primarily an idealist, Péguy maintained that idealism and social action were parts of the same whole. He devoted his efforts as a young man to the defense of Alfred Dreyfus—a Jewish officer unjustly accused of selling French military secrets and purposely victimized by the forces of reaction in France to discredit the republic which had made his appointment possible. This celebrated incident caught up all France in a crescendo of passions; it divided the republicans and the counter-revolutionaries, the Catholics and the defenders of *laicization*—and eventually the Dreyfusards and the anti-Dreyfusards.

In the end Dreyfus was exonerated, and a vigorous anti-Catholic reaction set in. This, too, Péguy fought as unjust and intemperate, motivated by hatred and vengeance, not human justice. It was characteristic of Péguy that he believed the humanitarianism he cherished was the greatest treasure of France, that it was most nobly manifested by the French people whose heritage had uniquely prepared them for it. Thus Péguy linked humanitarianism with a sense of national obligation and patriotism. Significantly, he died as a common soldier in the first battle of the Marne in World War I.

The swirling currents of ideas from which French youth grasps its beliefs are evidently contradictory. The rationalism and reasonableness of Voltaire are imposed on the excitement or romanticism of Rousseau. The defiance of Alain is balanced by the stern appeal to conscience of Péguy. Running throughout is a lusty faith in individualism and pride in the excellence of the French spirit of liberty. Here and there—especially in Rousseau and Péguy—are strong undercurrents of the *mission civilisatrice:* "France understands liberty; with real liberty she is producing civilized men and women; it is her duty to light up the dark corners of the world where liberty does not yet exist." The gap between liberty and majority rule on the one hand, and resistance to authority and effective preservation of the "Rights of Man" through social action on the other hand, has not been easily bridged by the French Republic's philosophers. Nor can it be without attention to the mechanics of government and specifically to the problem of political representation. Perhaps this topic has not been emphasized by the republicans because anti-republican spokesmen and impatient revolutionaries posing as republicans have constantly crowded out or threatened the principles of liberty, humanism, and the "Rights of Man."

Competing for the minds of the young, which are officially subject to republican school teachers, are contemptuous voices denouncing what they regard as the excesses of the libertarians.

Inevitably their philosophies emphasize the mechanics of a government which will reestablish order, restore the moral teachings of the church and provide an atmosphere in which men of wisdom and sound judgment direct public affairs. There is little attractiveness in these so-called traditionalist ideas for the young. However, the same cannot be said for another school of philosophers which through the ages has appealed directly to the emotional reactions of the French. Hence the strength of the Napoleonic traditions, the popularity in some quarters of the arch conservative, antisemitic Charles Maurras, the phenomenal ability of action-groups to attract followers by promising hand-to-hand violence in the streets against the leftists. The inflexible reactionaries, such as de Maistre, who would have restored the church and the aristocracy to absolute power, have little currency, but two other apostles of the Right enjoy, even today, some popularity. Maurice Barrès, turn-of-the-century novelist, shaped a nationalist sentiment which built upon the splendor of the French past and the desire for vengeance against Germany that had animated many Frenchmen since the defeat in the Franco-Prussian War of 1870. Barrès turned his nationalism to the ultimately reactionary purpose of erasing individualism and political distinctiveness in pursuit of the greater goal of merging self with motherland. Inevitably, however, his novels were used by less scrupulous counter-revolutionaries as ideological support for the most sordid political adventurism. On a different plane, Marc Sangnier attempted with no immediate success, but with a zest which assures the popularity of his writings even today, to fuse the liberal social philosophies of the revolution with Catholic dogma. The earnest young men who founded the *Mouvement Républicain Populaire,* as a progressive, democratic party during the *Résistance* in World War II, had all read their Sangnier years before.

There is a tendency in France to divide the country between those who have attended the state schools with their heavy dosages of republican and democratic works and those far fewer Frenchmen who have matriculated in Catholic or private schools. This is a convenient differentiation to make, because the product of each school system may often be identified according to his politics. However, this is entirely too simplified an approach to the distinctions between Frenchmen, to the differences which make them not only politically quarrelsome but also often politically paralyzed. To a considerable extent the influences of all France's great writers are felt by all inquisitive young people. Furthermore, even if the intellectual upbringing of the French were sharply divided into two separate systems, both would contain contradictions and inconsistencies within their own camp; there would be no one pure faith, no single dogma on which all pupils would be nourished to the exclusion of other ideological influences.

Class Consciousness

The second great national influence affecting most Frenchmen is a function of the political cleavages which have torn the fabric of modern French society. To a certain extent it is also an outgrowth of the industrial revolution which hit France with full force in the latter half of the nineteenth century. This influence is a lively class consciousness. Social distinctions run sharp and deep, although less so now than before World War II. Observers of British life have often noted when one Englishman introduces another Englishman to a third, the latter will soon find the opportunity to ask the first, "What is he?"—by which he means, what does this stranger do? "To what class does he belong?" This is seldom necessary in France; not only are the French able to spot differences of social standing by a variety of indices, subconsciously known to most of them: dress, accent, speech habits, gestures, and in the case of older people, physical stature—but in most instances the Frenchman will aggressively declare his standing on the social ladder.

To say one is a member of the working class does in fact explain certain things about a Frenchman. It probably means, for example, that his home, if he is a city dweller, is in one of a few particular districts. It is highly likely that, if he is not a member of the Communist Party, he has at least voted for the party on occasion; he may or may not read *L'Humanité,* the party newspaper, but he surely is exposed to it daily. The chances are that he does not pay his union dues but identifies himself, nevertheless, with one of the three major French national unions, scorns the other two, and is at the same time a firm believer in a somewhat mystical principle on which he can talk at great length: the unity of the working class. He almost certainly has been neither to a university nor to a *lycée* (the French equivalent of the academic high school); more importantly, he is probably well aware that his children will not attend them either. As a matter of course he considers his employers, the business world in general, and very often the government, as an organized gang of exploiters. He is apt to dismiss them with the most withering disdain by an epithet suggesting that after all he can have nothing in common with them: "They are of the Right!"

The employer may well feel a corresponding sense of distance from his workers. He is apt to be rather proud that he is a bourgeois. He would not utter the word "bourgeois," because in the French social lexicon it connotes smug stuffiness and selfishness, not particularly attractive values. Nevertheless, he will compete for status symbols to prove his respectability to his neighbors with an intensity that is often destructive of other human sentiments. He will certainly assure his children that they will either have access to advanced education or a place in the family business. The chances are that he will have no scruples about his wife and children attending Mass, although he himself may be an indifferent Catholic. He may take the sweepingly inclusive view that all his workers are Communists, and hence that he owes them nothing save the minimum salary necessary to entice them to his premises. He probably regards government social legislation as dangerous concessions to the strength of the Communists, but feels that his business must be financially aided by the government as a necessary protection for himself, his class and France against the Communist menace.

The two men described above are, fortunately, stereotypes. Although exaggerated, however, these descriptions do demonstrate the typical attitudes of one group of men about their relationships to another. There is more than dislike and strangeness between the two. Fear, mistrust, and contempt are the strong emotions involved in these human divisions. We have already discussed the depth of feeling between the pro- and anti-revolutionists in France, but here we are by and large dealing with men who both accept the republic—although they would, if they could, adapt it to serve their own interests. What may have begun as simple political differences in the eighteenth century (when many employers supported the *ancien régime* and most workers were republicans) has now moved into a more complicated phase as economic distinctions become more important. The industrial revolution brought to France a whole new range of social injustices, around which the bitterness expressed by only a few of the more radical revolutionists in 1792 took on meaning for broad sections of urban populations. The early French Socialists grafted their blueprints for a collectivist society onto the already existing philosophy of republicanism which had primarily demanded political equality. Eventually, the whole strand of republican thought divided itself between the political reformers and the socio-economic reformers. Later, of course, the foreign import, Marxism, was to find a ready-made market for its tempting merchandise in France.

The social gulfs in France are growing less sharp and ugly. However, what is most important to the Frenchman is the fact that he believes a social gulf exists and is proud to place himself on one side of it or on the other. Thus the Frenchman overlooks the fact that in the postwar world the Marxist conception of an exploited and pauperized proletariat is no longer a wholly valid image. By the same token, the employer tends to ignore the fact that his most successful competitor has pushed ahead by adopting a new industrial psychology which, if costly in terms of payroll and plant investment, pays off in terms of new orders and profits. Political reflexes in France have a resistant quality. There is a tendency for the Frenchman, despite the objective realities of his situation, to stick stubbornly with the eternal political verities on which he has traditionally depended for ideological comfort and emotional satisfaction.

French society is obviously far more segmented than the simple division: labor/bourgeois. In the first place there are still vast numbers of peasants, ranging from the dirt poor to the very rich, but generally all suspicious of inroads by urban politicians on the rural areas' traditional domination of French political power. Moreover, France is over-commercialized. There are proportionately more economic units engaged in the distribution of goods than in any other modern industrial nation. In these circumstances it is obvious that overall profits from commercial enterprises are divided into tiny fractions. Many *commerçants* are little better off than the meanest paid factory worker, and yet the political and economic impulses of this large social group will frequently vary widely from those of their blue-collared peers who are dependent on the payrolls of large and impersonal economic institutions. Finally, there are millions of civil servants in France, where many sectors of the economy are operated by the state. Their pay may be miserable, but their relations to their employer are of a special character, designed to insure their job security and to assure them some personal dignity in retirement in a manner often unknown to the average industrial worker.

Thus, the easy generalization about class lines dividing Frenchmen is difficult to maintain convincingly. Clearly the gulfs are not based primarily on economic differentials. The most ferocious rightists in France at mid-century are the weakest of the shopkeepers, who wear the traditional blue overalls associated with the working class, who serve and live in the gray, proletarianized slums of the cities. Many of them are moved, not by the Communist propaganda of their customers, but by the basically selfish appeals of semi-fascist demagogues who promise them freedom from taxation, the removal of government price-fixing, and low interest on government loans. They scorn the well-dressed business man as much as their Communist customers. Aware the chances are small that they will become true bourgeois entrepreneurs, they seek protection and insulation from the competition of big business. They do not find it unnatural in certain circumstances to accept alliance with their Communist customers and neighbors in obtaining this protection. Once again political imagery keeps this occasional alliance of convenience alive: "The government is a formidable force which the monied interests use for their own devices. Both must be defended against—in extreme conditions they must be destroyed."

Peasant Origins

The third great factor influencing much of French society and its political life is the closeness of its people to the soil. Although one small slice of Parisian France is universally acknowledged to contain the world's most urbane and sophisticated people, the great majority of Frenchmen either were born on the farm themselves, or are only one generation removed from the peasantry. Until World War I, more actively employed workers were engaged in farming or in the distribution of farm products than were involved in industry. Curiously, France boasts many of the oldest cities in Europe, but apart from Paris all of them are fairly small, and a substantial number were born and still exist as commercial centers for the marketing and distribution of farm products.

Unlike other modern advanced nations, France does not have sharply differentiated regions where either farming or industry dominates vast areas, almost to the exclusion of the other. Some parts of France are more highly industrialized than others, but extensive agriculture is found in almost every section. Of the ninety-two departments into which metropolitan France is divided, agriculture plays an important role in all but a handful. Until the period between the two world wars the economies of more than half the departments were predominantly agricultural (since then the scale has been tipping in favor of industry). An economic map of France still shows only occasional blotches of gray, indicating industrial agglomerations, against a large background of green. Large farms—or estates—can be found in France, but the vast majority of peasants operate very small establishments, usually by themselves. Only about one farm in six employs hands in addition to the family.

The problem of smallness is compounded by the division of farm lands. Many peasants own farms fragmented into odd-shaped and even non-contiguous parcels that are the result of generations of dividing and subdividing the family heritage. In the latter part of the nineteenth century the fragmentation of land had reached such ridiculous proportions that two important consequences resulted: movement to the cities picked up and births in peasant families began to fall off sharply. A peasantry which saw little purpose in further dividing its lands kept its heirs to a minimum, and thereby contributed significantly to the decline in the birth rate France experienced between the two world wars.

The psychology of the small French peasant has been cruelly described in Émile Zola's pungent but exaggerated novel, *La Terre*. The children of an old farmer, unwilling to await the distribution of the lands coming to them, finally murder their father. The life depicted is harsh and crude—selfishness is the primary motivating force of the characters. The protagonists are completely obsessed with the soil, with the limits it imposes on the course and prospects of their lives, with the necessity to defend their share of it and their right to it against members of their own family as much as against strangers, almost as they would defend life itself. Here we have another stereotype, overdrawn to the point of caricature, but useful nevertheless. The average peasant is accustomed to smallness, to the possibility that what is small will, if he is not vigilant against all outside pressures, become even smaller. Preserving what one has becomes a primary goal; change contains potentially terrifying danger; the outside world is probably the gravest threat to the minimum stability of the present. In short the peasant is inner-directed, his horizons are limited by his fears.

As we have seen, vast numbers of Frenchmen have come from peasant backgrounds. They may now be fully urbanized—in the sense that they have no desire to return to farming—but they have not completely shed their psychological heritage. They have, in fact, infused their preconceptions of society wherever they have gone; peasant-originated attitudes dominate much of the middle and lower-middle levels of French society, the small shopkeepers, artisans, mechanics, workers in commerce, and even large numbers of France's army of civil servants. The peasant roots of so many Frenchmen do not stamp them indelibly as members or sympathizers of one political group or another, nor necessarily range them on one side or another of the intellectual barricade represented by the concept of the class struggle. They do, however, moderate the effect of other divisions and of other strong political influences. They are a great force working for skepticism, for the privatization of interests as opposed to the concern for public problems. Above all, they turn the Frenchman away from politics in general: politicians and the political world are on the outside, are strange, and therefore are potentially dangerous.

The peasant complex, as this orientation might be called, is a strong element in that much discussed French characteristic, individualism. Every writer on France finds it necessary to observe sooner or later that the French are highly individualistic. Some commentators find comfort in this observation because they regard it as support for the argument that the large French Communist Party can never be as effective as its size in numbers would suggest. Since the French are so individualistic, the argument goes, the party cannot count on its members to behave in a disciplined and hence responsive fashion. There is, no doubt, some truth in this, but the largest Communist strongholds in France are, by comparison to other political and social groups in the country, fairly homogeneous, and more responsive to discipline than any other element in the population. The intense individualistic tendencies of many Frenchmen are not as evident in the party ranks as elsewhere. However, the peasant orientation keeps alive in much of the rest of the population a sense of individualism that is strange to American experience. Where we equate individualism with a dynamic, almost ruthless go-it-alone drive, the French peasant displays his individualism in a static defense of what is his against all outside challengers.

The Church

Curiously enough the church cannot be considered a universal influence or a unifying element in French life. France is normally considered a Catholic country, but it would be inaccurate to say that most Frenchmen are Catholics. Many are baptized by the local priest at birth; somewhat fewer are confirmed, married or buried by the church. Weekly attendance at Mass and observance of other devotional obligations are quite different matters. In only a few departments, particularly in Brittany and the German-oriented regions of Alsace and Lorraine, are a majority of the people indeed practicing Catholics. In most departments the number of real believers, as they are called, falls well below 50 per cent. In some of the working-class quarters around Paris only one adult in twenty describes himself as a practicing Catholic. Generally more faithful in their religious duties are the 800,000 Protestants in France, who include some of the country's most powerful business and banking families.

Ever since the revolution the Catholic Church has been a center of controversy, its survival in the republic causing more divisiveness than unity in the society. For the most part republicans have scorned the church as a revival of the *ancien régime,* and the more militant among them have adopted aggressively anti-Catholic views to demonstrate the vigor of their republicanism. The central domestic political issue of the Third Republic was the surviving influence of the church; as we have noted, strenuous efforts to preserve the lay character of the national school system often completely occupied the foremost politicians of the Left. Even today the gulf between believers and nonbelievers has not been bridged. In 1960 some 10,000,000 Frenchmen signed a petition to eliminate the program of state subsidies to Catholic schools that had been forced through a reluctant legislature by a strongly conservative majority. Nevertheless, fear of the church's power is by no means as emotional as in the past; a Catholic party has successfully established itself as a progressive rather than a conservative force, and Catholic trade unionism has won a respected place in French labor. On balance, however, it must be concluded that the average Frenchman tolerates or ignores the church; he does not regard Catholicism as a primary force in his personal life, and is satisfied as long as it does not become such a force in the life of the nation.

Conclusions

Enough has been said now to indicate that simple explanations of French political behavior are insufficient and dangerous. For a long time it was popular to draw a line between Frenchmen as either of the Right or of the Left—some more rightward or leftward than others, but each subject finally to specific classification. There are, of course, Frenchmen who accept and Frenchmen who reject the revolution—as we saw in Chapter 1. To pigeonhole a Frenchman so peremptorily, however, is unfair. He may be touched by other important influences—by the peasant complex, by fixed notions on the class struggle, by the pervasive and heavy hand of the universal French school system which, although designed primarily to make him a republican, very often produces more nationalistic sentiments than republican ideals. The sharp distinctions which one might expect to emerge from the Frenchman's historical mindedness become blurred by competing and often conflicting influences. Out of the matrix comes a variety of political types; furthermore the process continues to evolve. At mid-century it is possible to say that Right and Left have lost much of their meanings in the French political lexicon. A detailed examination in the chapters which follow of the character of the de Gaulle regime and the supporters it has attracted will amplify this hesitant conclusion.

3 - The Constitution

As it is in most countries, in France a constitution is a means of legalizing a new social or political situation which is sufficiently different from past conditions to necessitate a redefinition of the political-legal base on which the authority of government and the rights of the people are anchored. Implicit in this definition is the existence of dissatisfaction with previous arrangements—dissatisfaction strong enough to justify defiance of the most basic legal contours of the state. In France this defiance has often been expressed first by violence, with the adjustment of constitutions following shortly after. This is by no means a uniquely French phenomenon, but it has happened more often in France than in most Western nations. Surprisingly, no strong sense of public cynicism has developed in the light of rapid constitutional changes. Indeed, even the most unscrupulous political demagogues are cautious about bringing down on their heads the charge that they have violated the existing constitution in any way. They may be demanding the dissolution of the republic, but they will attempt to justify themselves: "My actions are within the law—the government which tried to repress me overstepped its limits"; or "My action (against the state) is legal because the old constitution has been invalidated by the incumbent government which has illegally violated it." Perhaps the explanation for this devotion (if only an intellectual devotion) of the French people for the rules which guide its government is to be found in the national penchant for seeking principles in all things.

André Siegfried once remarked that an Anglo-Saxon mother admonishes her son "to be good" while a French mother invariably pleads with her young "to be reasonable." This is the earliest and simplest appeal to an intellectual approach to the problem of organizing life. It is but a few steps away, however, from selecting principles for the whole society, and enshrining them in a document with a special dignity of its own. A constitution is, after all, a collection of principles. As such, it holds a special meaning for the French, habituated by their schooling and their family upbringing to reasoning out the logical essence of a situation. One might go further and say that a constitution is especially appealing to the French not only because it is a collection of principles, but because it is an abstraction. It exists primarily in the minds of men; for the most part its force is purely intellectual. That is to say, it can be interpreted, appealed to, even denounced, but the actions involving it are for most Frenchmen only mental responses usually requiring the adoption of a particular philosophic stand or position. The constitution cannot feed him, warm him, or house him, but it can comfort him by providing an orderly frame of reference from which he can deduce his own philosophic judgments about the nature of his role within the state, and his relationships to the government or to his fellow citizens.

Another aspect of the Frenchman's relationship to his constitution is apparent in this curiously intellectual attitude. To compose a constitution or to identify personally with a constitution is a declarative act, an affirmation of faith and intentions. Since this in turn is an unusually significant step for the Frenchman he is often inclined to regard his identification with stated constitutional principles as a sufficient personal commitment to the state or government. To go further, to accept and undertake the continuing responsibilities of citizenship implicit in the enshrined doctrines is by no means as important. In short, positive intellectual gestures often outweigh sustained, vigorous support of political ideals in daily life.

To the Frenchman then, a constitution is necessary, not simply because public affairs are made more tidy by the fact of having one, but because he can orient himself by examining his own views on it. That which is unconstitutional is particularly odious because it threatens the logic, the reason, the consistency of the whole. This attitude prevails even if the Frenchman in question heartily disagrees with the constitution in force. He will almost certainly insist, if the existing document passes into limbo, that a replacement for it be sought as quickly as possible. Such a predisposition explains some of the skepticism which greeted General de Gaulle's stern admonishments to undisciplined army units in January 1960 and to mutineers in April 1961. His own action of declaring that the orders of the Pétain government were not binding on him at the moment of French surrender to the German *Wehrmacht* in 1940 was unconstitutional—if perhaps justifiable on other grounds. Twenty years later the general seemed to be implying in his rebuke to the army that acts in defiance of the constitution were inadmissible unless their end was to create a truer legitimacy. This is thin philosophic ice on which to base a theory of power. It has long troubled the French. The Declaration of the Rights of Man adopted in 1793 contained the famous Article 35: "When the government violates the rights of the people, insurrection is for the people, and for each sector of the people, the most sacred of rights and the most indispensable of duties." In slightly altered form this clause reappeared in the first constitution of 1946, later rejected (for other reasons) in a popular referendum. In practice this ringing assertion has meant that if an act of defiance or revolution succeeds, it will thereby achieve its own legitimacy; if it fails the authority challenged need not hesitate to declare the action criminal. Only the French are sufficiently concerned with the necessity of defining their rights, duties, and delimiting the role of power in their society to the point where they find it rewarding to solemnize an age-old conundrum into a principle of civic obligation.

This is a dilemma which follows de Gaulle to the present day. On the one hand, he has been associated with the unconstitutional—or at least highly irregular—undermining of two governments, in 1940 and in 1958. On the other hand he is keenly aware of the special reverence for constitutionality so deeply felt by many Frenchmen. Thus, he must treat the new constitution with respect and reserve. He is, in other words, embarrassingly identified with an awkward document which, although it is known as his own, is subject to further cutting, snipping, and alteration only at great peril. There are, of course, means of revising the constitution in perfect legality, but an overuse of the amending process would amount to an admission that the job as done originally was inadequate to the task at hand. For whatever else it is, the constitution of the Fifth Republic is very much the creature of one man—Charles de Gaulle—although it was actually committed to paper by the pen of Michel Debré, who subsequently became the first premier of the republic's first government. The constitution of the Fifth Republic is a reflection of a basic Gaullist conception which in itself is a partial denial of republicanism: a careful scrutiny of the new constitution and of the explanatory statements made by those defending it shows that the state, or the French Nation as many Gaullists prefer to call it, stands a little to the side and above its government. The distinction is never clear, but what does seem obvious is that the old concept of republican government monopolizing the expression of public will and disposing of the full power of that will is dead. There appears to be an ambiguous vestige of power in the new constitution which is rooted in the very heart of the country—in the perpetual nationhood of France, distinct from the popular will or any function of transitory popular sovereignty.

In essence the constitution of the Fifth Republic is an attempt in words to assign the power and authority of the state or nation to a steward (in this case the president) and to divide the remaining elements of power and authority between popular institutions. The steward cannot be described by that useful old cliché, the servant of the people—although all the other officers and institutions created fall in this category. The steward is not a servant because he does not receive powers from the public—he maintains a set of powers that have their origins not only in the public will, but also in the historical fact of French statehood, the grandeur of the nation, and the totality of authority and prestige Frenchmen living and dead have accumulated for their motherland.

Clearly there is an aspect of mysticism in all this. There are no specific articles where the precise philosophy of sovereignty here described is laid down. In fact the constitutional document, itself, contains only a few doctrinal assertions: "France is a republic . . . its principle is government of the people, by the people, for the people"; and in a separate article, "National sovereignty belongs to the people." Both statements echo similar articles in the 1946 constitution, which was vastly different from de Gaulle's. The distinctiveness between new and old constitutions is to be found not in their preambles but in the assumptions and relationships of power implicit in each, and the interpretations offered by those charged with the exercise of these powers. For de Gaulle's constitution this process is by no means complete at this writing. The general has molded and remolded some of the original work since its ratification, but there have been few formal amendments. Presumably the evolutionary process will take a long time, and will be supplemented from time to time by formal amending sessions. Be that as it may, the constitutional instrument now in force has a character, albeit a still evolving one, which distinguishes it radically from previous French constitutions.

Perhaps the simplest method of describing the nature of de Gaulle's constitution is in terms relative to the past. The purest form of popular sovereignty attempted by the French was the popular assemblies of the convention period—when legislative decisions were made at what amounted to mass neighborhood rallies. Although short-lived and highly unsuccessful, this was a practical approximation of Rousseau's popular will in action. In modern times the closest parallel was the still-born first draft of the 1946 constitution. Its principal focus was a popular assembly equipped with such formidable powers that the premier and his cabinet would scarcely have had political identities of their own. The Assembly was to share its powers neither with an executive nor with another legislative house. The voters rejected this version in a dispirited referendum, and a few months later adopted the constitution which survived until 1958—a much more balanced instrument permitting greater flexibility to the premier and restoring the institution of an upper house, the Council of the Republic, as a limit on the power of the Assembly. By contrast the constitution of the Fifth Republic, although paying lip-service to the theory of popular sovereignty, in fact moves considerably away from this theory toward one of national sovereignty. Adoption of de Gaulle's constitution represents a decisive victory for that sector of French opinion which has traditionally sought to lay the ghost of Rousseau. Rousseauistic theory is not yet fully discredited, but de Gaulle, Debré and their collaborators have at least scored a clear triumph over the champions of majoritarian rule, the legal theorists of the Left, who have always insisted on the monopoly of power by a popular assembly, delicately attuned to the whims of the popular will.

There have been attempts by defenders of the new constitution to justify its character as a great step forward in perfecting an instrument for the transmission of the Rousseauistic general will. Their argument runs that the powerful president provided for in the Fifth Republic will serve as a true voice of the French people. Separated from the private and special interests thrusting their demands on the Assembly, he will be able to determine what is in fact the valid interest of the whole people. However, this conception of the role of the presidency is not Rousseauistic; Rousseau in rather ambiguous terms tended to emphasize popular sovereignty and to belittle the scope and responsibility of the executive agent in government.

What is crucial in the Rousseauistic synthesis is that the popular will is essentially correct in its estimate of a given situation; accordingly its will must be expressed as directly as possible to avoid distortion of the true will. The principal features of the new French constitution separate the presidential authority from the public and its will, even on the occasion of the president's election. In fact, General de Gaulle, in interpreting the nature of the president's office, has intimated that it must be sufficiently removed from politics to enable the incumbent to make his decisions in terms of the best interests of the nation —which obviously may or may not be what the public will would dictate at any given moment. The president thus becomes a sort of Napoleonic steward of the national interest, not the mouthpiece of the general will.

To emphasize the new direction in French constitutional development the Gaullist drafters sharply divided the functions of the legislative and executive branches. One does not derive its authority from the other—although there are some interacting relationships which are not dissimilar to the checks and balances of the United States Constitution. The concept of republican authority welling up from the public and receiving its expression in a parliament intimately tied to hundreds of home constituencies and closely controlling an executive that is in fact only a reflection of the legislative body—all this has been wiped away in the Gaullist constitution. Choosing the president is a separate process from electing a parliament; furthermore the choice is not made through direct election but by a cumbersome college of local mayors and city councillors too large to congregate in one place and debate its choice, too small to allow the development of firm party lines or disciplined party backing for specific favorites.

Not only does the constitution of the Fifth Republic separate legislature and executive, it also provides for two distinct executive officers—the president and the premier, the latter chosen by the former. The premier's role is to determine and guide the policy of the government, but since the Assembly plays only a secondary role in his selection and can remove him only with great difficulty he is normally independent of it and, at least insofar as the first government of the Fifth Republic is concerned, more powerful than the legislature. Whether in future governments under different presidents the premier will become more a creature of the Assembly than of the president is problematical. There are certainly provisions in the constitution whereby the Assembly could harass a premier having only lukewarm backing from his presidential sponsor, or if the president himself were weak. Over the long run much will depend on which practices and precedents established by de Gaulle become part of constitutional writ and which are rejected by lesser men or rust away from disuse.

The great reversals of past constitutional form explicit in the charter of the Fifth Republic have been described by its authors as a modernization of out-of-date practices. There is considerable truth in this. The assumptions underlying the constitutions of the Third and Fourth Republics were no different from those on which the First had been based: legislatures existed to protect the people from the ambitious wielders of national executive power. By far the most effective way to do this was to parcel out small doses of power (which could be withdrawn at any time) to governments performing minimum essential tasks of day-to-day operations—governments which were not really dangerous because they were legally only committees of the all-powerful legislature. But even the most slavish devotee of juridical niceties would have been forced to admit that the actual conditions of government under the Third and Fourth Republics were a far cry from the politico-legal images inspired by these comforting views of assembly government, so dear to the professional republicans. The weakness of the executive—or rather the predominant power of the legislature—complicated the task of implementing an effective and consistent program of government action to the point where premiers were often forced to demand special emergency powers to secure legislative agreement for even the simplest policies. The complexities of industrial society in mid-twentieth century were beyond the capacities of governments without power, tenure, or freedom of action. Those executives who chose to defy the realities of legislative power in the Fourth Republic and displayed vigor and determination—men such as Pierre Mendès-France—tried to fortify their own authority by appealing to the public over the heads of the legislators. In so doing they risked rousing parliamentary hostility, and over the longer run, political isolation.

A paradoxical by-product of this system of eighteenth century government in the twentieth century was the growth of bureaucratic or administrative power largely unchecked by popular controls. To some extent this development has troubled all modern states; it is a simple expedient for accommodating the insistent demands on government to involve itself more and more in the economic affairs of nations. In France the expansion of bureaucratic power, begun under the Third Republic, hit full stride after the Liberation and installation of the Fourth Republic. If premiers were weak by virtue of the strict surveillance imposed on them by suspicious legislatures, bureaucrats—charged with the day-to-day implementation of policies—often operated with much greater freedom. Worse, however, they were in France by and large unaccountable to the public. The Assembly of the Fourth Republic, aware of the inconsistency between the theory of an omnipotent legislature and the alarming reality of a paralyzed government, acquiesced in the growth of administrative power. Non-elective government officials implemented policies that were adopted by the legislature only in skeleton form. One bitter example of this development was the delegation of civil powers to the military establishment in Algeria. Eventually the Fourth Republic became a victim of one of its servants when the army abetted the Algerian settlers in the 1958 coup that put an end to one Republic and gave birth to another.

The Fifth Republic's assertion that it is characterized by a strong presidential executive, an executive that does not draw its strength from popular assemblies, is indeed a sharp departure from past constitutional practice. But the most distinctive characteristic of the Fifth Republic's Constitution, the one which makes it unique in the republican history of France, is not the impressive strength of the executive so much as it is the absolute reduction of the functions and powers of the legislature. The principal organ of the popular will no longer holds the center of the political stage—at this writing at least.

The limitations on the legislature—discussed in detail in

Chapter 5—appear on their face to be chastisements meted out against a body that has misused its power in the past. Constitutional restrictions are placed on the length of the legislative sessions, on the freedom of deputies to initiate legislative action, on parliamentary budgetary power, on the subjects which legislation may encompass, and even on the Assembly's freedom to determine its own financial needs. Of these restrictions one of the most galling to deputies of the first legislature was the shortness of the sittings, because the Government, as the cabinet and administration is called, exercises wide powers when the legislature is in recess. In point of fact, the executive has a clear advantage in the distribution of power, and under special crisis conditions it can usurp even those attributes of power specifically granted to the legislature by the constitution. Furthermore, the existence of such emergency conditions is determined by the president.

As the executive is divided between the president and the premier, so the legislature has two parts—the Assembly and the Senate. However, the drafters of the Fifth Republic, not content with the absolute reduction of the Assembly's authority, have continued the trend initiated by constitutional revisions in the last years of the Fourth Republic, by giving new dignity to the Senate—making it almost coequal in legislative responsibility, although its membership is indirectly elected. By this balancing of powers the Gaullists have returned to a notorious provision of the Third Republic, one insisted on by the monarchist majority in 1875 to minimize the influence of the popularly elected Chamber of Deputies. However, in the 1870s the framers wished to checkmate the power of the Chamber because they feared radical spokesmen would eventually dominate it. In 1958 the same system was adopted not because radicals threatened to overflow the Chamber, but rather because the Gaullists were disenchanted with the past behavior of the institution as a whole and the comportment of its members, whether of radical, moderate, or reactionary persuasion. As a matter of fact, proportionately more "Left-leaning" senators were elected to the first Senate of the Fifth Republic than to its Assembly.

Another body blow at the old concept of legislative supremacy in the government of the Fifth Republic is the provision of what appears to be an entirely independent organ, the Constitutional Council. Traditionally in republican France, Parliament not only dominated the other institutions of government, but its decisions, expressed in legislation, were unchallengeable. Thus, there was no room for judicial review as it is practiced in the

United States. Establishment of the Constitutional Council points the way to a modest experiment in judicial review. Actually the Council membership, although including some parliamentarians, is heavily weighted in favor of the executive branch and includes, among others, all former presidents of the republic. It functions as a sort of umpire between the legislature and the government. In a conflict or dispute over the division of powers between the two, for example, as to whether a matter is properly handled by legislative action or decree action by the government, the Council may be called upon to decide; its rulebook is the constitution, or at least what the membership of the Council believes the constitution dictates.

It is, as yet, too soon to judge whether Frenchmen will accept the political philosophy underlying the creation of the Constitutional Council. More than any other institution of the Fifth Republic, perhaps, it is an explicit recognition of a reversal in traditional French constitutional theory. The sole justification for its existence, apart from a few purely housekeeping responsibilities, such as assuring the regularity of elections, and determining the constitutionality of treaty texts, is to define the relationship between separate instruments of government—and thus presumably by its decisions to clarify these divisions and enforce their existence. Because it is independent of the legislature, it has succeeded so far in its young life in serving as a watchdog over a disgruntled parliament, impatient with unfamiliar restrictions on its traditionally all-powerful role. However, the Council, simply because it is both a novel institution and an independent one, could in time become either the tool of an executive anxious to expand its already impressive share of authority, or an early victim of an indignant legislators' revolt against the stringent constitutional division of powers.

A final, sharp departure from the political France of the past is the abandonment of the concept of the unitary state. For generations the principle on which France conducted its relations with its overseas territories was that effective power emanated from Paris. In practice this principle was applied either literally or conservatively depending on the political circumstances of the moment in metropolitan France, but the essential relationship always remained the same. The system of political affairs was predominantly French, whether a French commissioner made every decision for a dependent people in Africa, or whether local political leaders in ceremonial native regalia were admitted to the National Assembly in Paris on a full and equal footing with deputies from Bordeaux and Quimper. Local units of the empire did break away from France from time to time, but those that did so had to force the issue themselves—the possibility that there might be some attraction to disassociation with France was never, at least legally, admitted. In fact French citizenship and participation in French political affairs were considered the pinnacle of achievement for a formerly dependent people. This policy—called assimilation—was largely developed under the Third and Fourth Republics, and will be discussed fully in Chapter 10. Only in the last two years of the life of the Fourth Republic were arrangements adopted which recognized the need for advancing the national character of dependencies. Even then, however, the fiction was maintained that the territories involved were being offered the opportunity to prepare for autonomy, not independence.

The constitution of the Fifth Republic establishes a French Community as the principal link between metropolitan France and its overseas elements. The Community, at least on paper, appears to be a far cry from the British Commonwealth, but in practice it may be drifting into this sort of loose association. Although the constitutional articles describing the Community are vague at best, and although they are undergoing constant adaptation and interpretation even as this volume is being printed, one aspect of this institution suggests something of the new political philosophy at work in France. The metropole, that is, continental France, is no longer the source of all power and authority which its overseas associates are privileged to share, and in whose legislative and executive organs they may be invited to join. Rather, in the new constitutional theory emerging, France now stands as a power in itself, and so do other countries, which may or may not exercise the advantage open to them of establishing ties with France. Some characteristics of the old assimilation policy still remain, and indeed some overseas territories remain in a dependency status but, by and large, the emphasis in the present arrangements is on voluntary associated relationships, in which power is divided (albeit unequally for the most part) between France and those peoples anxious to cooperate with France. The only organs of the Community provided in the constitution are an Executive Council, a Senate, and a Court of Arbitration. The president of the republic also serves as president of the Community. These organs are primarily designed to fix and to regulate the relations between the French government and the autonomous or independent states of the Community.

Moreover, Article 86 of the constitution offers any Community member state freedom to leave the Community—a privilege not hitherto considered admissible in France.

Conclusions

Frenchmen have caustically described their new constitution as a *mélange*—a mixture or jumble. It is certainly that, and perhaps for this reason it puzzles the French. As we have noted, the French are accustomed to seeking principles or systems of logic in their patterns of life or thought. Their new constitution does not, even after the most careful study, fit into any single philosophic mold. Its various parts do not mesh together and produce a system which can be neatly labelled "presidential regime," "responsible parliamentary government," "liberal majoritarian democracy," or what have you. It includes elements of all of these and many other systems of government. It contains a preamble of principles adopted word for word from the preamble of the constitution of the Fourth Republic—the very system whose shortcomings made it possible for the Gaullists to sweep it into the dustbin of the past with hardly a whimper of nostalgic regret from the French people. Many of its important areas are left for definition in the future by the process of passing organic laws—statutes that supplement the constitution, and assume its legal force when passed by the legislature. At this point, then, the curious hybrid is still unfinished.

Furthermore, new anomalies may be grafted into it at any time by the amendment process. Amendments can be initiated either by the president, on proposal by the premier, or by members of the legislature. After an amending bill is prepared and debated by the two legislative bodies it can become law in one of two ways. First, it may be passed by both assemblies and then confirmed in a national referendum. A simpler method is also provided, which some critics regard as easily exploitable by a strong president with a submissive parliamentary following determined to tailor the government to his own specifications. If the president so decides, he can submit his amending bill to the two houses of the legislature assembled in congress, and it shall be considered approved without resort to a referendum if it receives three-fifths of the votes cast.

In short, the constitution is in a state of development. Its fluidity is enhanced by a number of factors: the looseness of many of its provisions, the continuing necessity of implementing some articles by the passage of organic laws, and the ease of the amendment process. Furthermore, changes and adaptations are more, rather than less, likely to occur because of the mixed origins of various parts of the constitutional system. Frenchmen will not for long resist the temptation to impose an overall philosophy on their new *pastiche,* and in so doing will probably strengthen some articles at the expense of others. Most important, the constitution is still recognized as the instrument of President de Gaulle—the French world of politics remains at this writing susceptible to the powerful influence of his authoritative voice. There is every reason to believe he will continue to regard the constitution as an imperfect document which is only one of a number of means by which he hopes to reconstitute the grandeur of France. Under certain conditions he may feel it demands adjustments as do other elements of his regime or other aspects of his overall polity.

4 - The Executive

The government of the Fifth Republic was tailor-made for General Charles de Gaulle. As such it provides almost unlimited scope for the development and exercise of the executive powers it was presumed he would hold. This not-surprising feature of the government is, however, complicated by the curious expedient of providing a dual executive, whose two elements have unequal powers. However, any full understanding of the workings and significance of these executive institutions can at this writing only be incomplete. The new government is still under test, and the development of executive institutions has been confined under the circumstances to two quite distinctive individuals.

General de Gaulle, the first president, is unique among Frenchmen both as a figure in world history, and as a political leader who spurns politics. His personal qualities have been deeply imprinted on the office of the presidency as it has taken shape so far in the short life of the Fifth Republic. But it is precisely the uniqueness of his personality and his position in

French life that makes any description or analysis of the office he holds highly tentative. No other Frenchman is likely to bring to the presidency the national prestige of de Gaulle, nor is any other Frenchman likely to be comfortable with the vast array of powers developed by the general. Successors will find it difficult to resist the impulse either to scale down informally the powers of the presidency or to use them in such a completely different fashion as to distort the present nature of the office.

As de Gaulle is a unique figure in the presidency, so Michel Debré is in the premiership. The first occupant of this office largely devised his own powers and those of all the other elements of government. Debré has, in other words, a strong personal stake in the success in its original form of the machinery he designed. No successor is likely to feel himself as inhibited as Debré has been in elaborating ways and means of making the government's rather cumbersome machinery more flexible.

Presidents and premiers were also features of the Third and Fourth Republics. It is the difference between the old concept of the presidency and the new version which makes the constitution of the Fifth Republic distinctive. The monarchical majority of the original Assembly of the Third Republic, unable to agree on an occupant for the throne, compromised on a president as the repository of national sovereignty, with the expectation that the office would soon be abolished when a proper king became available. It was only natural under these circumstances that the first elected occupant of the presidency was a somewhat regal figure in his own right, a representative of traditional political conservatism who was himself a confirmed monarchist. This was Marshal MacMahon, a professional soldier who had taken part in the brutal crushing of the revolutionary Paris Commune in 1871. MacMahon's name is important to French constitutional history because of his clumsy attempts to expand the original president's functions by dissolving the Assembly and calling for new elections which, he hoped, would produce a more satisfactorily conservative majority. Both he and the precedent he sought to establish were destroyed. The republicans rose angrily against what they considered a usurpation of power, drove MacMahon from the presidency, and thereafter followed the example made explicit a generation later by Georges Clemenceau, who was to become the leader of France during World War I. When asked which presidential candidate he supported, "The Tiger" replied: "I vote always for the most stupid." From the fall of MacMahon in 1879 until the fall of the Third Republic in 1940 no president ever again dared presume to dissolve the legislature; few would have had either the inclination or the personal strength to attempt it. Under the Fourth Republic it was not even constitutionally possible.

THE PRESIDENT. The very office of the presidency under the Third and Fourth Republics became a symbol of the republican drive to fetter and impede executive authority—a drive which subsequently was carried on against the office of premier. At the same time, because it was at least theoretically the pinnacle of political status to which a Frenchman could aspire, competition for the honorific title of President of the Republic often developed into bitter parliamentary battles. One result of these circumstances was the evolution of a set of practices whereby mediocre men were elected to a largely ceremonial office, usually after the spilling of considerable political blood in a protracted public spectacle which disenchanted the public at large. There were of course serious attempts made to change this pattern. During the inter-war years of the Third Republic, Clemenceau, and later Aristide Briand, a skillful foreign minister and a principal architect of Western efforts to achieve peace in Europe by nonaggression treaties and disarmament, were induced to offer themselves as candidates for the presidency. Both were defeated by lesser men—largely on the grounds that they were too strong, or that their personalities would inevitably force them to overstep the limited functions of their office.

The one important task assigned to the presidents of the Third and Fourth Republics was that of choosing new premiers. Although this seems not unsimilar to the responsibility of the British monarch, in fact the problem was much more complex. Never was there a simple choice as in the United Kingdom between two possible candidates who were the leaders of the two major opposing parties. French presidents, when tackling the task of government reconstruction after a crisis or an election, were confronted not only with a host of competing parties, but very often with rival contenders for power and leadership within a single party. Accordingly, the president had to be a compromiser and balancer of conflicting political interests—a negotiator skilled in weighing one contender's capability of putting together a coalition of parties against another's—and sometimes a salesman with the capacity to induce one man of strong principles to head a cabinet containing varied political elements. Inevitably, then, the successful president was himself a graduate of the rough and tumble school of parliamentary struggle and compromise.

Occasionally, the president could contribute to national stability and even enhance the institutions of the republic by refusing to be stampeded into the early choice of a new premier during a government crisis, or by guiding the parties toward a settlement of their differences in the interest of producing a workable majority when the country was desperately in need of leadership. Such a man was Vincent Auriol, first president of the Fourth Republic, whose tact, patience and doggedness helped steer France out of several debilitating political crises. By and large, however, the president was only a necessary catalyst whose function was to minimize political chaos when it threatened to cripple government operations completely. He could not lead the way toward new directions of overall public policy or substitute his strength for the weakness of others.

DE GAULLE AND EXECUTIVE POWER. The views of General de Gaulle on the authority of the national executive were developed not out of any doctrinaire attachment to a particular philosophy of government—although his parents had been monarchists—but from a critical analysis of the workings of the Third and Fourth Republics. He saw the impotence of the presidency as a fundamental fault which exposed France to grave dangers when crises threatened. In an appearance before the Constitutional Committee considering the draft text of the constitution of the Fifth Republic, de Gaulle told the trenchant story of President Albert Lebrun's role during the June days in 1940, when the French government was agonizing over the decision of whether to capitulate to the German invaders or to remove the government to North Africa. Lebrun never intervened nor even pressed his views on the government ministers, whose paralysis was matched only by their desire to abdicate. De Gaulle told the committee that Lebrun explained to him later in a pitiful interview: "I was not responsible . . . if I had been responsible, if I had been able to carry legitimacy with me, I would have left for Algiers." The irony of this little story lies in what de Gaulle did not say: If Lebrun had failed to take the legitimate government of France to Algiers and there set up an effective and continuing resistance to the German invaders, the general himself, had not stood by idly. On the contrary, by escaping to London and setting up a government-in-exile, he had acted illegitimately. What he had taken with him was not the constituted authority of the French government, which in fact had been forfeited to the enemy, but the more ephemeral entity best described as French honor. On this wisp de Gaulle built a powerful political force that reestablished French authority in the overseas empire, reconstituted a military establishment, demanded and partially obtained a voice in the councils of the Allied Powers, and when France was liberated, installed virtually without hindrance a provisional government in Paris.

We have already discussed the concept of national stewardship held by de Gaulle, and the rigid views of constitutional correctness and republican legitimacy maintained by most Frenchmen. Clearly these two beliefs were bound to conflict when the war ended, the Germans had departed, and France found herself under the care of one man with a demonstrated contempt for legitimate authority and an unshakably powerful personality. The French people, although duly thankful that the imposing general had expunged much of the disgrace of 1940, were notably uncomfortable with the justification he offered for his conduct. To base the authority of a government on the survival of national honor smacked too much of a political philosophy in which the origins of sovereignty were found in military power, in the successful defense of national existence by the force of arms. Although national honor was an appealing phrase to the average patriotic Frenchman, it was simply not a substitute for the more mundane sources of national legitimacy to which republican politicians had been philosophically accustomed. Leaders of the pre-war political parties and of the *Résistance* movements came into increasing conflict with the intransigent chief of state. For his part, the provisional president, who had once described himself as a "reluctant democrat, but a democrat, nevertheless," did not conceal his anxiey about the pronounced trend in the constituent assembly toward resurrection of a comfortably familiar weak executive. Suspicions about de Gaulle grew; by some he was openly branded an authoritarian, by the Communist Party, a fascist. He departed the provisional government before the constitution of the Fourth Republic was written or adopted, but he did not abandon the image of what his own role in relationship to France had been during the *Résistance*. Nor did he desist from pressing on the French people his concept of what an executive should be, although his suggestions went unheeded. The architects of the Fourth Republic adopted almost unchanged the institutions of the Third, which the public apathetically accepted.

The purpose of this little detour into recent French political history is to demonstrate how radically the nature of executive institutions and their theoretical origins have changed in a little over a decade and a half. The de Gaulle notion of executive power has been accepted by the French people, although one suspects the personality of the general was more appealing to the public than the character of the office he filled. In explaining his own position in relation to the nation in 1960 the general went unchallenged when he declared: "the legitimacy of the French Republic, *which my person has incarnated for three decades,* remains." De Gaulle appeared, on the surface at least, to be majestically sweeping away the twelve-year life of the Fourth Republic. Probably, however, he did not mean to imply that the Fourth was an illegal interlude between his provisional government during the war years and his return to power in 1958. Rather this statement seems to fit his own conception that national authority is best expressed and implemented in a powerful executive, and that as the sole occupant of such an office, once under unusual emergency conditions and again twelve years later with the public sanction of a legally accepted constitution, his person provided a repository of national authority—albeit an inactive one for part of the period.

The somewhat mystical qualities of the presidency as envisaged by de Gaulle are cloaked in a few short ambiguous phrases in the constitution, phrases which appear susceptible of infinite interpretation and reinterpretation: "The President of the Republic shall see that the constitution is respected. He shall ensure, by his arbitration, the regular functioning of the public powers, as well as the continuity of the state. He shall be the guarantor of national independence, of the integrity of the territory. . . . When the institutions of the republic, the independence of the nation, the integrity of its territory or the fulfillment of its international commitments are threatened in a grave and immediate manner and the regular functioning of the constitutional public power is interrupted, the president shall take the measures required by these circumstances. . . ." Imprecise as these provisions are, they far outweigh the powers or responsibilities assigned to any other institution of the government. When combined with the more specific delegations of authority granted the president, discussed below, they constitute an executive power unparalleled in French history since the second Napoleonic period.

Executive Power

It is convenient—although not always possible—to distinguish two types of power entrusted to the president: those which become operative under extreme emergency conditions, and those which are associated with the normal conduct of public affairs. In both areas the scope of the presidential powers has been expanded enormously. Furthermore, it should be remembered that under existing constitutional arrangements the premier, who is selected by the president, is also subject to dismissal by the president. Thus the premier can be (and at present certainly is) the creature of the president, faithfully carrying out the directives of his patron, who may thereby control almost every piece of government business.

The constitution gives quite extraordinary power to the president in the field of foreign relations. Written into the constitution at the insistence of General de Gaulle, this power represents a clean break with the past. Although it may have been justified when adopted as necessary to afford de Gaulle free exercise of his enormous personal authority in dealing with the rebellion of the Algerian nationalists, the primacy of the president in foreign affairs will probably remain as a fixed feature of the Fifth Republic. Already it has resulted in the diminution of the premier's responsibilities in this field, and has turned the office of foreign minister into a largely technical and administrative post.

Extraordinary emergency powers are granted but not specified in Article 16 of the constitution, which states simply that under unusual circumstances hazardous for the republic the president may take such measures "as are required by these circumstances." Before assuming the power authorized in this article the president is obligated only to consult with the premier, the presidents of both legislative chambers and the Constitutional Council. Any measures he promulgates under these powers must at least be discussed with the Constitutional Council. The National Assembly is assured of its survival during the president's exercise of these powers since it cannot be dissolved as long as Article 16 is in effect.

So far, Article 16 has only been invoked once in the life of the Fifth Republic. This was on the occasion of the mutiny of the generals in Algeria in April 1961, when Paris experienced several days of agony and apprehension lest the military revolt against the government's Algerian policies spread to the metropole. De Gaulle interpreted his powers under Article 16 broadly —using them to create special military courts, apply censorship, terminate the existence of some newspapers by fiat, and in certain circumstances to suspend the normal liberties of citizens so as to facilitate police searches, seizures and confinement. The president requested these powers for an indefinite period, thereby raising a wave of protests from the Left, and visions of dictatorship throughout a much broader spectrum of French opinion. Just how far a president could go under the authority of Article 16 is not yet clear, but some critics have already pointed out that even constitutional revisions might be possible with such a sweeping license.

As indicated earlier, however, the normal day-to-day functions of the president and the emergency powers which he holds are not always readily distinguishable. He is, for example, charged with making appointments "to the civil and military posts of the state." Under any circumstances this is a necessary prerogative of the chief executive, but in a government where day-to-day business is presumably conducted by a premier, it seems an unusual power to bestow on the chief of state. In actual fact, of course, de Gaulle has used this authority to name the men who control Algerian policy—the success of which is vital to the very survival of his regime. The president also acts as commander of the armed forces and presides over the High Council of National Defense. Again, in normal circumstances this might appear an unusual power bequeathed to the president at the expense of the premier, but because of the persistent Algerian rebellion which has plagued the Fifth Republic the president's direction of this sensitive body that determines all national defense and securities policies is not entirely unnatural.

The president may wear many hats in one day. Thus he can begin the morning by presiding over the Council of Ministers, where broad issues of public policy are discussed and the position that the Government will take before Parliament is determined, decrees agreed upon, and from time to time appointments made. Later he may be found propounding a change in strategy for the war in Algeria at the High Council of National Defense. In the afternoon, he may deliver a message to the Assembly, receive the newly appointed ambassador of a foreign country, or preside over a meeting of the prime ministers of the French Community.

From this catalogue of presidential powers and functions, one simple conclusion may be drawn: If he wishes to, the president can exercise influence on or authority over every principal institution of the government. By far the most important and sensitive is, of course, Parliament. While it may be true that at the moment these words are being written the military establishment wields more political power than the Parliament does (see Chapter 10), this is not a normal state of affairs for France and probably will not continue after the Algerian problem has been resolved. But the relationship of the president to Parliament will be a permanent feature of the regime and for some years, at least, will probably be a source of friction and political strain. The great bulk of the French public is habituated to parliamentary government, awkward, paralyzed, and feckless though it may have been in the past. For this very reason, and because of the traditional republican suspiciousness of any threat to the power of Parliament, the president's leverage on Parliament is bound to be regarded critically not only by the deputies and their parties, but by broad segments of the public as well.

The power to dissolve the Parliament is potentially the biggest stick in the president's arsenal. Only mild restraints limit the president's prerogatives in this field: he must consult the premier and the presidents of the Assemblies before acting, although he is not bound by their advice; after elections are held to replace Parliament, he cannot use his dissolution power for another year. In short, the president holds the power of life and death over Parliament. The deputies must be prepared to face up to this ultimate threat if they wish to stand on a principle with which the president differs. It is by no means clear whether this power is directed at intransigent parliamentary majorities or at a premier defying presidential leadership. When de Gaulle opened the first session of the Fifth Republic's new National Assembly in late 1958 he indicated that in his conception, at least, it was aimed at the Assembly. In introducing the members of the Government (that is, the ministers) to the deputies, he remarked grimly: "This is your Government, gentlemen; you will have no other." In addition to his dissolution power the president, much in the manner of the American chief executive, may impose his views on the legislature by official messages which are not subject to a debate. If it is not sitting, the legislature may in fact be called into special session to hear presidential messages.

The president's authority to press his views and exert his influence on the official institutions of government is matched by his right to communicate directly with the people. Apart from the normal privilege of a chief executive to discuss his policies before the public in speeches and written pronouncements, the president may under certain circumstances submit major issues to a public referendum. This constitutional provision has been assailed by some critics as a dangerous weapon which could be used by an unscrupulous president to exploit his personal popularity in a situation of conflict with Parliament to the disadvantage of the deputies. However, any such action by the president is limited to issues of a clearly constitutional nature or those dealing with a treaty, and the proposal must be initiated either by the premier and ministers or by motion of the two houses of the legislature. Thus, captious use of the referendum as in the Napoleonic period is not likely under the Fifth Republic, although there is no denying that the referendum procedure could be employed in lieu of the normal amending process to engineer large scale constitutional changes in defiance of parliamentary wishes. In practice, however, President de Gaulle has used the referendum process not out of any solemn regard for constitutional niceties, but to reinforce his political position. On the occasion when structural changes in the French Community were necessitated by the departure into independence of several African territories and when no strong political opposition to the adjustments was foreseen, the simple amending process was used. However, when de Gaulle sought public sanction for policies that would end French domination of Algeria in January 1961, and needed to demonstrate to bitterly opposed rightists who were threatening to destroy his regime the strength of his popular backing, he invoked the referendum procedure.

The Premier

In the halcyon days of the Third and Fourth Republics political life centered around the premier. The struggle for power in France was complex because the victory of one man or one political force was rarely complete, and even less frequently long lasting. However, the prize was always the same: the office of the premier, or as the post was confusingly called under the Fourth Republic, president of the Council of Ministers. The rapidity with which premiers were invested and deposed led one pundit of the postwar years to describe the office as equipped with its own built-in revolving door. Because politicians who had once held the post were permitted to retain the title after stepping down, the French political world was crowded with personages officially addressed as *Monsieur le Président*. Debates in the

Chamber of Deputies often gave the impression of colloquies between a college of presidents. Almost all the leaders of the principal parties—save the Communists—had held the post at one time or another; deputies who had not yet achieved the purple controlled their behavior and guided their voting records so as to do nothing which would prejudice their chances in the future.

Ironically enough, the title better describes the functions of the premier under the Fifth Republic than it did under the Fourth. Because the President of the Fourth Republic was largely a ceremonial chief of state, the president of the Council of Ministers not only provided overall guidance to the government ministers, but combined in his office the normal powers of chief executive, and largely shaped the domestic and foreign policies of France. In the Fifth Republic, although considerable opportunity for an expansion of his functions exists, the premier's role has developed largely in the province of coordinating the activities of the government ministries. He heads the institution, new to the French constitutional lexicon, called the Government. The Government consists of the executive departments, and all their administrative apparatus. As a political institution, however, the Government is somewhat more than simply a collection of high political officers and their departmental underpinnings. It is also the body placed in opposition to Parliament, that is the organ which presents the official policy of the leadership of the country to the parliamentarians, solicits their approval and, in certain circumstances, can be destroyed by their disapproval.

THE GOVERNMENT. Curiously, the word Government as used in the French constitution is not precisely the equivalent of the same word as used in British parlance. First, the Government in Britain is embellished by the prestige and symbolic authority of the national sovereign: the prime minister is the Queen's first minister, the navy, Her Majesty's Royal Navy, etc. Moreover, the relationship of the Government to Parliament in Britain is not conceived of—at least in theory—as one of opposition. The Government, essentially a committee of Parliament, is more apposite than opposite to that body. The Queen and her Government, in other words, perform their duties and direct the affairs of the nation in conjunction with Parliament. To be sure, in practice a faction within Parliament can make damaging attacks on the Government, or so embarrass the Government that its political officers feel compelled to resign—but the continuity of Her Majesty's Government remains; theoretically the sovereign's stewards have merely been replaced.

In France the officer symbolic of French sovereignty—the President of the Republic—is not part of the Government, although, of course he may control it completely as the British sovereign can in no way do. Furthermore, the Government, although alone responsible to the Parliament, is not a part of the legislature, and in fact the two institutions have been made constitutionally incompatible. Thus, when a Government is chosen, its members must, if they have seats in either house of the legislature, resign those seats. Should a Government lose the confidence of Parliament, it is possible—although by no means certain—that its replacement would be drawn from among those deputies whose opposition had caused the collapse of the previous Government. At that point, however, the deputies appointed to the new Government would be obliged to sever their connections with the legislative bodies. Herein lies one of the most startling innovations of the Fifth Republic. By separating the Government from the representative institutions of the public, but nevertheless making it responsible to the legislative bodies, a potential conflict is created. The premier and the Government do not derive their authority from the benevolence or cooperation of the parliamentarians,[1] but must, notwithstanding, submit to the criticisms and ultimately to the official displeasure of the bodies with which they work. On the other hand, the Government has no independent strength by which it can enforce its authority in relations with the legislature. The premier does have formidable powers, as we shall see in subsequent paragraphs, but the greatest share of his prestige and authority is derived from the backing of the President of the Republic. Lacking this, he and his Government are at the mercy of the deputies.

POWERS OF THE PREMIER. We noted in Chapter 3 that some provisions of the French constitution are so written that they suggest the framers shared a deep distrust of legislative power. In addition, we have just observed that the institutional arrangements of the Fifth Republic appear to be based on the assumption of conflict between executive and legislature. The powers of the premier are, in keeping with this philosophy, designed to give the custodian of this office every advantage in his relationships with Parliament. The power of the Government in the field

[1] The premier is chosen by the president. The Fifth Republic's first premier, Michel Debré, although he was not constitutionally obliged to do so, solicited and received a favorable vote for himself and his Government from the legislature before assuming his official duties. Whether his action constitutes a precedent that will bind his successors is, of course, unclear.

of legislation is at least equal to that of the British cabinet operating with a large parliamentary majority. Indeed, the freedom of action enjoyed by the French Government in some ways is even greater than the British because its superiority over the legislature —including a recalcitrant one where the premier and his ministers are confronted by a large and hostile minority—are guaranteed not only by specific constitutional provisions, but also by the Constitutional Council, and if he is willing, by the president's intervention in behalf of the Government.

The role of the premier in the legislative process under the Fourth Republic has been described as that of an "unwelcome solicitor," who championed his policies in direct competition and rarely on more than equal terms with other powerful voices and interests represented in the Assembly. All this has been changed. In the first place, the overall business of the legislature has been reduced, and that of the Government increased. A sharp distinction between those matters which may be considered in the realm of law—and hence debatable in the Parliament—and those which are only subject to the decree of ordinance-making of the Government now exists; this distinction will be discussed in greater detail in Chapter 5. Second, the premier has been given a commanding position in the initiation and conduct of legislative business. Thus the Government's program is normally spelled out in a series of Government bills submitted to Parliament for its approval, and these have priority over all other pending legislation. While the legislators may in their turn inscribe propositions of law for consideration, no such proposition is acceptable if it either reduces public funds or includes the necessity of raising additional public funds—a safeguard against indiscriminate private lobbying in public affairs carried over from the practices of the Third and Fourth Republics. To all intents and purposes, then, Parliament is restricted to the discussion of Government bills. Significantly, even as its bill is being debated, the Government of the Fifth Republic may intervene to indicate what parliamentary committee will prepare it for floor debate, or may demand a vote on the whole bill rather than on each of its articles. Third, in case the two houses of the legislature are unable to agree on the final text of a bill, the Government can actively intervene to secure a compromise favorable to its conception of the text in question. Finally, financial legislation submitted to Parliament by the Government must be acted on within seventy days; failing this it becomes the subject of the ordinance-making power of the Government and goes into effect regardless of the attitude of the Parliament.

The key to the relationships between premier and Parliament is, of course, the ultimate threat held by Parliament to discharge the Government by withdrawing its confidence. Under the Third and Fourth Republics this was a relatively simple matter. The possibility of legislative disapproval on a major policy matter hung over the head of every premier and his cabinet. This generally served to inhibit the executive's freedom of parliamentary maneuver and in addition set clear limits in advance on the scope of the political program which the premier could set before the Parliament. Under present arrangements the legislature's potential for overturning Governments has been vastly reduced—or, perhaps more accurately, the premier and his cabinet have been given better defenses to protect themselves against the wrath of the deputies. Initiative for testing Parliament's confidence in the Government can come either from the premier or from Parliament itself. The premier may, if he so decides, declare a Government bill or a simple statement of general Government policy a matter of confidence. The National Assembly of Parliament must, if it wishes to challenge the life of the Government, produce a motion of censure signed by at least one-tenth of the total membership. This motion is considered adopted only if it receives a majority of all the members, and only favorable votes are counted. Moreover, the signers of the original motion cannot introduce another motion of censure during the same session, and hence are assumed to be constrained from acting captiously or out of momentary pique. The same procedure may be followed directly by deputies wishing to challenge the Government on any issue. However, in the case where the premier presents a bill or statement of policy on which he stakes the life of his Government, his text is considered adopted and approved even if it fails to pass the National Assembly, as long as the motion of censure which it provokes also fails.

Conclusions

A review of the pattern of relationships between the two-headed executive and the legislature suggests at least one principal conclusion about the political philosophy underlying the Fifth Republic. The executive is assumed not only to be correct in its judgments of what public policy should be, unless positively contradicted, but there is also a strong presumption in favor of executive continuity and stability. The interrelationships of the executive institutions generally enforce these precepts, presumably on the supposition that insulation from the tempestuous whims of special interest groups is a necessity for the leader of France since it cannot be guaranteed to the legislature. Nevertheless, the complexity of the executive institutions and their relations to one another complicate the firm establishment of these principles. Much depends on the personal predilections of the president. If, for example, he wishes to steel the resolve of his premier—as General de Gaulle has shown himself constantly prepared to do—he may warn the legislature that in the event it revolts against the Government it will be dissolved. On the other hand, a less forceful president, unwilling or incapable of asserting his authority might allow his premier and Government to drift aimlessly between his own directives and the challenges of an irate, uncompromising legislature. Thus, there is potential for the development and strengthening of a completely new concept of executive authority in France, or for the beginnings of debilitation of the novel institutions of the Fifth Republic.

5 - The Legislature

The step-child of the Fifth Republic is the legislature. In the past, French political life swirled around the ornate lobbies and paneled chamber of the Palais Bourbon, seat of the National Assembly stolidly situated on the left bank of the Pont de la Concorde. Not only was the greatest share of political business of the Third and Fourth Republics conducted in the lower house of Parliament, or Chamber of Deputies as it was also called, but on more than one occasion political battles were fought in the streets surrounding the Palais, as Frenchmen sought by direct action either to influence the legislature or to destroy it. The Chamber came to symbolize the republic and all its works; it finally became the focus of all criticisms aimed at the shortcomings of French politics. Spectacular careers were fashioned by mediocre men who spent a lifetime learning and perfecting the intricacies of political behavior as traditionally practiced in the Assembly; others less fortunate, or less skillful, were frustrated because they were unable to avoid being identified with the system. On the other hand, the Chamber sometimes experienced dramatic moments in the competition between great orators, immersed in critical issues and exercising almost total freedom of debate.

Perhaps because it was the arena where the "Rights of Man" were first enunciated and defended, the Assembly became in time the repository of Republican legitimacy—in theory the cockpit where the representatives of the people jousted for public recognition of their views. In the eighteenth and nineteenth centuries the highest duty of the deputy was to preserve the rights and liberties of his constituents against the encroachments of potentially tyrannical state officers. Inevitably confusion over rights and privileges developed: the deputies became more and more parochial and tended to regard their function as the defense of advantages which had accrued to their district by circumstance, natural good fortune or government action. From protectors of civil liberties the deputies were slowly transformed into the champions of vested and often purely local interests. The relationship between the legislators and the premier and his ministers, however, remained essentially the same. The ministers were constantly called on by indignant legislators to justify or explain actions of the government or its bureaucrats which threatened the individual dignity of the Frenchman or his sacred economic preserve.

The mark of the promising premier was his ability to deflect the demands which poured in on the government for the extension of special privileges, or to blunt the biting criticism of legislators who regarded the government as the epitome of obscurantism and the plunderer of local treasure. At the same time the premier who wished to survive was constantly forced to nurse along the coalition that constituted his majority, pleading with his own ministers not to lead the attack against him, while compromising the integrity of his legislative program in order to maintain the cohesion of his cabinet. To compound his difficulties the premier was often obliged to submit the various planks of his legislative program to hostile committees, whose chairmen were usually more anxious to enhance their own careers by brilliant critiques of the legislation under question than to contribute to the forward progress of public business. Perhaps most important was the fact that the Chamber could, virtually without fear of reprisal, yank the rug from under any premier by defeating legislation on which he had staked the existence of his government, or could force his resignation without a formal vote, simply by letting it be known that certain initiatives which he wished to take would not be welcomed.

The domination of the legislature over the premier and his government was almost complete—only once in the life of the Fourth Republic did a premier dare to use the power available to him to dissolve the legislature. His action so angered some of his colleagues in the Assembly that he was not only forced out of his own party, but for several years thereafter was virtually unable to reestablish political contact with many erstwhile party comrades.

In all this there was, however, a supporting philosophy to which the parliamentarians of the Third and Fourth Republics clung doggedly. Since the Revolution the enemies of republicanism were popularly believed to be lodged in havens where they could exercise influence disproportionate to their numbers. These havens were the church, the bureaucracy, and the military. The French executive was suspected of sheltering pockets of antirepublicanism in its military establishment and government ministries. Thus, harassment of government operations could be justified as a republican virtue. Moreover, the faster the pace of government change, of the rise and fall of cabinets, the greater the opportunities for numerous deputies to win the coveted title of minister—a device not only satisfactory to the professional politician, but justifiable on the democratic (and familiarly Jacksonian), grounds that any man, no matter how humble, could aspire to high office. This theory was often embellished to include the notion that no specific set of skills, no particular personal attributes were required for the conduct of public business. In practice, the primary qualification necessary to win appointment to a cabinet post, or even to the premiership, was often the number of parliamentary colleagues that the candidate could bring with him to the coalition that a new premier was trying to build. Thus, there developed a large pool of deputies in the Palais Bourbon who were potentially *ministrable,* that is, good material for adding to any cabinet, simply because they controlled blocs of votes and had never in the past made themselves personally noxious to the premier of the moment.

We have noted before that the system had many obvious faults, but that inevitably practices grew up which tended to minimize the worst effects. The growth of bureaucratic power and the tendency of the legislature to deliver whole areas of its legislative responsibility to the authority of ministers regulating by decree have been discussed. Throughout the life of the Fourth Republic more fundamental adaptations of the system were considered from time to time, but few were accepted as constitutional revisions by the legislature. Many proposed changes concerned the stability of governments, and the longevity of premiers. A few minor corrections were made in the last years of the Fourth Republic, notably, newly elected legislatures were shorn of the privilege of challenging the life of a government more than once in the first eighteen months of their terms. For the most part, however, the deputies held jealously to their monopoly of power, and continued to keep the government on the defensive. As we shall see, the framers of the Fifth Republic not only reversed the entire relationship between legislature and government, but incorporated into the constitution itself some of the informal legislative practices that had developed in the past as a means of obviating the most awkward consequences of legislative domination and executive instability.

The Organization of the Legislature

The two houses of Parliament in the Fifth Republic are the National Assembly—the popularly elected lower house—and the Senate—the indirectly elected upper house. The formal adoption of the title Senate for the upper house to replace the Fourth Republic's Council of the Republic was eyed with misgivings by some Frenchmen who felt it represented a return to the much-criticized Senate of the Third Republic, where powerful rightist politicians had entrenched themselves and sought to undo all progressive social legislation emanating from the Assembly. In essence, however, the National Assembly retains a slight edge in legislative power; for if there is disagreement over bills which are submitted successively to the two houses, and the disagreement persists for more than two formal readings by each house, and if a joint committee named by the Government for the purpose cannot compose the differences, the National Assembly then has the right to rule definitively on the substance of the matter. On finance bills, that is those either appropriating public monies or providing methods for the raising of public funds, such as tax legislation, the Senate is restricted to a fifteen day consideration of the matter before the process described above for the passage of ordinary bills goes into effect. Nevertheless, there is considerable room here for the development of powerful political forces in the Senate with which the Government may deal, if the premier finds the Assembly uncooperative.

Elections

Election to the 465-member National Assembly is defined by both "organic" laws—which carry more weight than ordinary laws—and by simple legislation that may be changed by parliamentary action at any time. When an election is called, all seats are contested. Under present arrangements (and in the past in France few election systems proved hardy enough to survive unaltered for many years), deputies to the National Assembly are chosen from single-member districts.[1] From the multiplicity of candidates normally running in a French constituency, the one receiving a majority of the votes cast is thereby elected. In most districts however, it is necessary to have a runoff—or *deuxième tour* as it is called—usually a week after the first ballot, because no single candidate will have received a clear majority on the first try. At that time the candidates receiving the least number of popular votes in the first ballot normally drop out, indicating to their supporters to whom they should throw their weight. In the second ballot the candidate with the most votes is elected, whether or not he has obtained a majority.

Senators occupy their seats for nine years; one third of the body stands for election every three years. They are elected by local colleges composed of officials from all the towns and municipalities of each district plus the members of the National Assembly from the district. Because the smaller towns have disproportionately more officials entitled to participate in the college in relation to the population they serve than do the cities with many thousands of inhabitants, the composition of the Senate tends to reflect the essentially conservative rural interests of France. Furthermore, because elections to the Senate must follow elections to the National Assembly, there is a tendency for local dignitaries with long political histories and strong personal influence, who have been defeated in their bid for seats in the As-

[1] This was the solution decided on by de Gaulle after much political squabbling over the merits of various plans, each calculated to aid the fortunes of a particular party, but all designed to weaken the Communists. De Gaulle, himself, who had had sad experience with the leftist-dominated Constituent Assembly at the end of World War II, personally rejected any return to proportional representation, the system by which its seats had been filled.

sembly by direct popular election, to enter the legislature through the less difficult doors of the Senate.

Both houses of Parliament convene for two short sessions annually—in all they are in session for only about half the year—a limitation of the legislature's normal free-wheeling functioning in a democratic society, which one cynical deputy has castigated as "enforcing sclerosis by inactivity." This limitation reflects the profound suspicion of an all-powerful Parliament shared by the framers of the constitution. In order to provide the Government with legislative support in times of emergency it is constitutionally possible for the premier to call special sessions, or a majority of the National Assembly may invoke the calling of an extraordinary session. However, the constitution authorizes the president alone to open and close special sessions of Parliament—a privilege which President de Gaulle has already interpreted as enabling him to refuse the demand of a majority of the National Assembly for a special session. To all intents and purposes, therefore, the executive can, if it chooses, ignore the legislature, except when it is sitting by right. The potential of this power is enormous in a governmental system where policy initiative is largely monopolized by the executive, and where the lines of communication between the executive and the public are naturally far stronger than those between the legislature and the public.

The Relationships of the Legislature to the Executive

It is perhaps an exaggeration to say that the critical function of the legislature has disappeared; nevertheless it has been greatly reduced as compared to the recent past. There are, of course, important mechanisms by which Parliament may seek to influence the government, or expose publicly what it feels to be the shortcomings of governmental action. Besides the normal processes of debate—in which, as we have noted, the premier may insist that his business have priority, and that his text be the subject of debate—one session each week must be set aside for a question period in which the deputies may question the premier and principal ministers. In actual practice, however, ministers are under no obligation to appear before the Chamber and have often avoided delicate issues by discreetly absenting themselves from the question period. As the parliamentarians have the right to question the Government ministers, so the latter have full access to both legislative houses. From this vantage ministers can apply acute pressure in behalf of the Government's program, but they do not do so from the intimate context of a shared membership in the legislative family since constitutionally the holding of a ministerial portfolio is considered inimical to the holding of a legislative mandate.

In line with this philosophy every candidate for the Assembly or the Senate is obliged to present himself to the voters along with a substitute who takes his seat, if the original candidate should be selected as a minister. This curious constitutional requirement, which gives evidence of the framers' toying with the theory of separation of powers, has succeeded in eliminating from the legislature some of its most effective and dynamic members. Moreover, since ministers need not be selected from Parliament, but can in fact be plucked from any profession, or walk of life, the Government team which deals directly with the legislature may include men who have no experience in parliamentary affairs—or as is the case with the high civil servants named to cabinet posts by de Gaulle—be virtually unacceptable to some members of the legislature.

The existence of a gulf between ministers and legislature is not unique to France. This difficulty has been singled out by constitutional experts as a potential weakness of the United States' system of government—and indeed some of the most ineffective administrations in United States political history could trace the beginning of their difficulties to the breakdown of communications between the President's department heads and Congress. Significantly, however, in the United States, Congress has almost always had the advantage in these conflicts. A Secretary of State under fire from a congressional committee may survive the committee's scorn, but his effectiveness as an officer of the President is thereafter limited. In France the Government minister who finds that his rapport with the legislature leaves something to be desired has powers of his own so strong that he can, if he chooses, shrug off parliamentary criticism.

Under the Debré Government, at least, the relations between Government and Parliament have been conducted almost as though hostility was the norm. The appearance of a minister on the floor of the Assembly or of the Senate presenting and defending the Government's business is under any circumstances a delicate affair. However, when the minister is a high-ranking member of the permanent civil service with little or no experience with the rules of the parliamentary game—and possibly with not much concern for representative institutions as such, since his career is not particularly affected by what they do—the gulf between executive officer and legislative officer can become dangerous. Worse, the Government, secure in its dominant position, may become impervious to the criticisms of the legislators. In brief, the relations between two of the most important institutions may decline either into open hostility or a negative aloofness on the part of one or both. Either situation could bring sudden and dramatic shocks to the body politic, especially if the frustration of the legislators suddenly turned squarely against the premier and his ministers, or even the president. In the French system as it has operated to date—because the only effective weapon open to the parliamentarians is the ultimate one of eliminating the Government by a vote of no-confidence, and because even this is a move which can be made only with great difficulty—there has been a tendency for both sides in the conflict to accept the situation which forces them into antagonistic roles.

Arrangement of the Legislature

While the British political system depends on the development of a close rapport between the Government and Parliament, it nevertheless assumes that the legislature will be sharply divided as between those forces who support and are indeed a part of the Government, and those elements who in different circumstances and if their opposition is effective, may one day anticipate controlling Government. This division between parliamentary forces is symbolized by the well-known architectural arrangements of the House of Commons, where two blocs of seats face one another, separated by the speaker's platform and the clerks' tables. The members of the Government sit on the front row of one bank of seats only a few steps away from the leaders of the opposition, who occupy the front row of the other bank. Thus, both parties appear to be poised to confront one another directly over their differences, their foremost spokesmen situated so that jousting can take place on a face-to-face basis.

In France the physical arrangements of the legislative chambers also symbolize the basic relationships among the elements of political power on which the system rests. Since no clear divisions run through the heart of the legislature as in Great Britain, all legislators are placed *en bloc* in a hemisphere or fan-shaped chamber, its benches facing the front, or narrowest portion of the fan, and rising in several tiers, each higher tier containing more seats. The first two short tiers on the floor level of the chamber are reserved for the Government ministers. Facing the whole fan is a complex dais containing the clerks' tables, a seat for the presiding officer, and the tribune from which speakers normally address the legislature.

The logic behind this arrangement is that the Government negotiates its business with the whole legislature. The deputies are arranged by party groupings from left to right in the chamber according to the political hue of their party—the Communist Party occupies the far left of the hemicycle, a small group of extreme reactionaries the far right. However, because almost any government will depend on support from a variety of parties or in some cases on segments of one party in combination with other segments or full parties, no sharp dividing lines can be identified separating the benches, except those that distinguish the ministers' seats from all the others. In short, the ministers are arrayed against all the legislators.

The presiding officers, or presidents, of both the National Assembly and the Senate are elected by their respective bodies, as are the bureaus which assist them in the conduct of their duties. These bureaus consist of several vice-presidents and secretaries, usually chosen with some regard for representation of the parties proportionate to their strength. Although some lip service is normally given to the necessity for impartiality in fulfilling these roles, the jobs are clearly political. The speaker, at least, has considerable power which he has won because of the strength of his party, or sometimes because of the crucial tactical position it commands between two or more antagonistic larger parties.

Hence, the presidents of both Chambers operate as partisans, but their partisanship is tempered by the necessity to keep legislative business moving, and by the very fact that they more than anyone else symbolize and represent the legislature in its relations with the executive. The president of the Senate fills temporarily the office of President of the Republic if it falls vacant for any reason. He does not, however, assume the functions and responsibilities of the president if the latter is merely absent from his post (e.g., if on on a state visit to another country). In such a case the premier may act for the president on certain matters; other business must simply await the president's return.

Legislative business is conducted, as in most legislatures, by committees. However, the constitution of the Fifth Republic limits the number of permanent committees of each Chamber to six. This represents a considerable reduction from the number of committees maintained in the past and was decided on as a means of reducing the power of the committees and their chairmen, which under the Third and Fourth Republics often lead the assault on Government legislation, and in many cases simply substituted bills of their own for the projects submitted to them, or routed Government bills endlessly through a maze of overlapping committees. By the reduction of the number of permanent committees the best training schools for aspiring political leaders on the national level have been dealt a body blow. Young deputies, who previously might have hoped to rise rapidly to fame and recognition by undertaking the important function of *rapporteur* (reporter) of a significant piece of legislation issuing from one of many committees, now must wait many terms before such an opportunity presents itself. Furthermore, if the occasion does arise, the Government, as we have seen, may decide that its text will be the only one considered by the Parliament.

Laws and Regulations

In the conflict between executive and legislature implicit in the workings of the Fifth Republic a notable and critical advantage accorded the executive is the constitutional distinction between the "law" and "regulation." Specific areas of interest are assigned to the preserve of the legislature; all other matters automatically fall into the category of regulation, which in essence means that the premier simply issues executive orders having legal force. Moreover, for limited periods the Government may request the authority to issue ordinances having the force of law in order to carry out its program. The difference between this practice and that of the past, whereby ministers were often accorded legislative authority in order to overcome the difficulties of the parliamentary system, is that formerly all legislative power was presumed to reside in the legislature. It could be temporarily bestowed on another institution or officer of government, but this in no way prejudiced the theoretical monopoly of legislative power vested in the people's representatives. Now for the first time the constitution defines what business belongs to the legislature and specifically removes vast areas of public business from its purview. While this is a radical departure from the political philosophy familiar to most adult Frenchmen, the division of powers is nevertheless a realistic recognition of procedures in effect for long periods of time under the Third and Fourth

Republics. The realism of this innovation is small comfort to French legislators, however, who are fully cognizant that it may no longer be possible to recapture functions now constitutionally denied them.

In general the law applies to almost all matters of internal or domestic affairs—civil rights, the privileges and obligations of citizenship, criminal codes and punishments, financial and tax legislation, electoral systems, and the relations of government with private business. In the matters of national defense, local administration, education, employment, regulation of unions, social security, and national planning, the legislature is restricted to laying down general principles; the details of which are filled in by regulations of the executive. Clearly, the enumerated areas of legislative power are not only divided between full and partial powers, but the whole range of legislative powers contains a notable lacuna: specifically in the matter of organization and reorganization of governmental institutions. It is in this sphere that the Fifth Republic's most ambitious, aggressive and sharply criticized activities have taken place. The executive has used its residual regulatory powers to shape and streamline the administrative apparatus of the state, particularly in respect to the armed forces and civil administration in Algeria. Furthermore, it has lavishly employed the leverage granted it by the constitution to secure passage of skeleton legislation from Parliament and then to flesh it out by ordinance.

The Economic and Social Council

Although the conservative framers of the Fifth Republic discarded much of the legal theory on which past representative legislatures had been based, they retained an institutional feature of both the Third and Fourth Republics that had been designed by radical reformers of the left. This is the Economic and Social Council, a large body of more than 200 members representative of all walks of French economic life: business, labor, civil servants, social workers, farmers, public health officers, etc. The Council, although minutely organized to include the voices of almost all significant occupational pressure groups, is purely advisory. Moreover, the Government or Parliament must solicit its opinion on pending legislation or regulation—it cannot speak out of its own volition. Delegates to the Council, who sit for five years, are normally chosen either by the Government or by the professional association, such as the union, to which they belong.

Legislative Power and Foreign Affairs

Despite the primary role of the president in foreign affairs, Parliament retains a veto on his treaty-making power. However, by implication the constitution excludes the involvement of Parliament in the negotiation and conclusion of "international agreements subject to ratification." Thus a president who interprets his powers vigorously may presumably carry on a whole range of international activities—in the fields of joint defense or the adoption of common policies with another country toward a third country, for example—without hindrance from the legislature. Finally, as we shall discuss in detail in Chapter 10, the legislature plays a role, albeit a minor one, in the affairs of the French Community. By contrast, the president is once again the dominant figure in the regulation of Community affairs as they affect France proper.

The Constitutional Council and the Legislature

In a constitutional system almost entirely new to the French, with specific authorizations of power divided among the various elements of government, with constitutional distinctions somewhat ambiguously drawn between the law of Parliament and the regulation of the executive, and with the presumption of executive-legislative antagonism hanging over all, the Constitutional Council provides an essential umpire function. The Council consists of at least nine members, named for nine-year terms, one-third of its membership being renewable every three years. Three councillors are chosen by the president of the republic, three by the president of the Senate, and three by the president of the Assembly. In addition, all former presidents of the republic are ex-officio members. The Council has two primary functions. One is essentially supervisory in nature—it supervises French elections and ensures the regularity of the referendum process. Moreover, all organic laws, i.e., those that pertain to the primary characteristics of government institutions, are automatically examined by the Council to determine whether or not they conform with the constitution.

The other function of the Constitutional Council, by far its most important, might be called its arbitral power. Any principal officer of the government, the president, premier, or the presidents of both Assemblies, may lay before the Council any law or the provision of any treaty which he may think is unconstitutional before its promulgation. Theoretically, because decisions of the Council are final and may not be appealed to any higher authority, they could be crucial if any single element of government determined to overstep its powers. Consistently, however, even the protection of the Constitutional Council favors the Government in its dealing with the legislature. If the Government feels that the parliament has legislated in a field reserved for executive regulation, the matter may be referred to the Constitutional Council for a definitive decision. However, if Parliament feels that the Government has invaded its prerogatives by issuing regulations in a field indicated as legislative, it has no similar recourse to the Council.

Summary

Any criticism in depth of the legislature of the Fifth Republic must, as must evaluations of the other principal organs of the government, await the passing of President de Gaulle. Not only were the legislative organs devised to fit the general's well-known preconception that unlimited parliamentary power gives rise to irresponsible maneuvering by political parties, but the executive was enormously strengthened to the disadvantage of the Parliament. It is unlikely that future legislatures will refrain from attempting to adjust the balance. However, while de Gaulle is in the saddle such efforts will certainly be strongly resisted, even though the resistance may increase the antagonisms between the institutions of government. Looking farther into the future it is possible to foresee the development of sharp political divisions—less over institutional jealousies than over fundamental political disagreements. The indirect election of the president will virtually insure that the office will remain a bastion of conservatism. The National Assembly, more receptive to changing popular political attitudes, will not always be the conservative chamber it now is. Thus there exists a potential for political frustration in the new system, especially if the various elements within it choose to play the game of checking one another's power, instead of coordinating their action toward agreed public goals.

In conclusion, it should be noted that for many Frenchmen the new reduced stature of the legislature is indisputably attractive. The game of politics as played by the Assemblies of the Third and Fourth Republics was by no means an inspiring spectacle. The desperate labors of responsible and dedicated men were often hidden by the more flamboyant and better reported histrionics of those whose machinations kept the legislature in a turmoil and sooner or later crippled virtually every government. The French public attitude toward the National Assembly as the formidable seat of republican power had, well before the birth of the Fifth Republic, slowly given way to a generalized contempt for Parliament—and even for parliamentary democracy. Perhaps a period of penance under the shadow of a strong executive will have a salutary effect on the occupational qualities of the French legislator. Under these stern conditions, and within a system where the advantage rests by definition with the executive, French parliamentarians may discover that new—or long unused—talents must be developed to force their way back into general public acceptance.

6 - Political Parties

Political parties in France are not organized to win a monopoly of power as much as they are to ensure the ideological purity of their followers. The French have insisted on flaunting the banners, the slogans, and the other paraphernalia of their beliefs so prominently and so aggressively that with a few exceptions their parties have tended to suffer from exclusiveness. Although each scorns compromise with other parties, in practice almost all are forced by their own weaknesses to accept compromise as a painful necessity of political life. The parties by and large are professional organizations with little or no public or amateur membership and participation; they are often transitory, in existence for election periods, quiescent otherwise. Exceptions to these generalizations about French parties exist, of course, and where they do they make significant inroads into the coherence and consistency of the party system as a whole.

It is time to recognize that, of all the institutions of the past criticized by those Frenchmen who ratified the constitution of the Fifth Republic, none was more vilified than the party system as it operated in Parliament. One consequence of the reaction against the party system is slowly becoming apparent. France is gingerly beginning the process of re-aligning its basic political sympathies, and of testing new systems of government that will give expression to these sympathies. The outcome of this period of experimentation and change is difficult to predict, and the general lines of any new synthesis that emerges may not be clear for some time. Hence, we shall concentrate in this chapter on those forms, patterns and habits of the parties and of the party system that still have life today and have such deep roots that they cannot be safely overlooked by those planning for the future.

The Parties and Ideology

Frenchmen, as we have seen in previous chapters, tend to wear their political and philosophical beliefs on their sleeves. By seeking to identify themselves with special political creeds they are striving to embrace consistent systems of thought which both rationalize their own behavior in everyday life and suggest personal objectives for the future. In a very real sense, therefore, ideological parties fill a strong need in French life. Some have been organized to embody the emotions and idealism emanating from a great moment in French history, others to preserve the ideas of some respected figure long since dead, still others to serve the interests of what is regarded as a precise and homogeneous class in French society—distinct from all other classes. The consequences of this particularistic division of party groupings are often startling. Thus, the staid and rather timid Socialists, now composed predominantly of government bureaucrats, wave the red flag of proletarian revolution and chant the *Internationale* with as much gusto as the Communists. They claim their party is the direct heir of the early French Socialist Party, a section of the Second Workers International which employed these same symbolic devices, and from which the Communists departed forty years ago, illegally misappropriating for their own use the badges of the true faith when they left. The ideologues of the Catholic MRP (*Mouvement Républicain Populaire*) insist on counting amongst the inspirers of their party the most liberal Catholic writers of the last half century, yet it is common knowledge that the views of these writers are shared by only a small fraction of the party following and a mere handful of its elected deputies. The Communists, for their part, associate their party with a myriad of historical events antedating the Leninist revolution in Russia, and claim as their forebears the same pantheon of immortals as the Socialists, from whom they are normally bitterly divided. In recent years, moreover, the political leaders of overseas and African France have drawn their ideologies from the liberal democratic teachings of French Radical Socialists of the nineteenth century; today the Radical Socialists in metropolitan France supply some of the more reactionary and colonialist-minded members of the overseas administration.

So, the ideals and symbols, the imagery of the past, linger on, although to those not personally identified with them they seem hopelessly outdated. However, even the evident contradictions and the historical anachronisms have a function in French life which is, at least from a narrow point of view, fruitful. When a Socialist orator who has been personally instrumental in the division of the trade union movement into Communist and non-Communist blocs thunders about "the absolute necessity of returning to the ideals of the past and of restoring the fundamental of working class unity," his Socialist listeners—although well aware that he would take part in no such thing—comfort themselves with the knowledge that this is what he would do if the world were perfect, and are reassured by his rhetoric that he "believes in the right things." Similarly the Radical voter with heavy investments in Algeria finds balm for his conscience in the deputy who speaks glowingly one day in the Chamber for the Rights of Man and the next day in his constituency defends the army's use of concentration camps in Algeria as a regrettable but necessary means of containing the Moslem nationalist revolution.

The difficulty in all this, of course, lies in the fact that French governments are normally based on a coalition of parties, since no single party can ever hope to command a majority of voters. Very often the basis of the coalition is an agreement among two or more parties with different philosophic outlooks to disagree publicly on certain basic issues, but not to raise these political issues in any recognizable form during the lifetime of the coalition. Naturally such a flimsy basis for cooperation is limited both by circumstances and by the degree of discipline which the parties can impose on their spokesmen. Once a back-bench deputy or a local leader raises an ideological question which jeopardizes the pretense of unity maintained by the national leadership the coalition is in trouble, because the rank and file will soon be spurred into asking even more embarassing questions. Discipline varies considerably among the French parties, ranging from the complete subservience imposed by the Communists on their troops to the freedom of conscience enjoyed by the Radicals on all but a few selected matters of party dogma. The most celebrated example of party discipline serving to hold a coalition together occurred early in 1947 when the Communists were still in the government of the Fourth Republic. In the vote on military credits for the continuation of the Indo-China War —a war in which the French were actively fighting Communist armies—the Communist Party ministers, who wished to remain in the government, blithely voted with their bourgeois colleagues in the cabinet for military appropriations and persuaded almost 200 rank-and-file Communist deputies in the Chamber to abstain.

But most parties cannot boast this degree of discipline because, apart from the Communists and Socialists, they lack permanent organizations which can be mobilized to take sanctions against mavericks who fail to follow the party line. Moreover, no perquisites, such as secretaryships and district organization jobs, controlled and distributed by national headquarters, exist for most parties. All parties, of course, do make some effort to preserve a national form and to enforce a minimum degree of uniformity of views on their elected representatives both on the local and national level. However, since most deputies of the Right and of the Center depend to a great extent on their personal popularity in their own home districts for election, disagreements with national headquarters over voting behavior are very often conveniently ignored. If a conflict of views occurs on a major issue in which the national leadership of the party is directly challenged by one of its members, some parties take the unusual step of expelling the challenger, usually after a party meeting has endorsed the move. Even this radical step, however, means little more than refusing the politician in question the use of the party label in future electoral contests. Again, because of the ephemeral nature of most party organizations, and even of party names, in many cases even expulsion does not loosen the offender's grip on his local fiefdom. He need only adopt a new label and confidently await his return to office by the faithful.

Clearly the doctrinal rigidity of the parties is more institutional than personal. A good number of the foremost political personalities in France are themselves quite flexible and adaptable men who have attuned themselves to public pressures and local needs over a period of years, as have the successful politicians of any country. Because there is no constitutional prohibition against the holding of two or more elected offices, the French deputy with a national reputation often serves concurrently as the mayor of his home town or as a member of his municipal council. Edouard Herriot, over forty years in the Assemblies of the Third and Fourth Republics, was for an even longer period mayor of France's second city, Lyons, as well as national chairman of the Radical Party and minister and premier in a number of governments. Such careers—and there are many not unsimilar—operate to create personal machines rather than effective party organizations.

However, from time to time, especially when the nation is involved in a political crisis or has passed through some profound political upheaval, even the most well-heeled personal machine may be threatened by the momentary appeal of a new movement. Thus in the 1958 elections which were called to fill the first Assembly of the Fifth Republic, scores of candidates were swept into office by the simple expedient of riding General de Gaulle's coattails. Very few politicians outside of the Communist Party chose to differentiate their beliefs or platforms significantly from the general's. Of those who did only a tiny handful were elected. However, even this dramatic display of political power did not produce a strong, monolithic party to serve as the active expression of de Gaulle's own philosophy. To be sure the party founded at the time, the *Union pour la Nouvelle République* (UNR), has a definite form, a national headquarters, a platform, and even some local branch offices in the larger towns. Its national bureau was in fact unified enough in 1960 to expel one of the party's founders, Jacques Soustelle, when he publicly differed with the president's Algerian policy. But what the UNR did not have and has not developed since was a broad pattern of beliefs, apart from devotion to de Gaulle, acceptable to a large segment of Frenchmen. As such it can anticipate considerable success while it shares the general's prestige. Once he has left the scene, however, it is evident that the party's cement will crumble.

Hence, like most political groupings of the Right and Center, the UNR is an impermanent movement containing diverse elements who might flake off at any time when personal circumstances seem to warrant defection. Already there has been some desertion occasioned by the inability of several UNR Deputies to follow the general's lead on colonial and Algerian policy. It is important, finally, to recognize that the indiscipline of large parties is frequently a function of French individualism. New groups are constantly formed to give recognition to minor philosophical differences between political leaders. Unless their credos touch the French public consciousness deeply, the new parties in turn become sectarian groupings, surviving purely for their own sake, and with only illusory control over their public spokesmen.

Some French parties have a peculiar double character, a fact which has contributed to the nation's political instability for generations. Extremist parties of both Left and Right, although represented in Parliament and generally accepted as legitimate organs of popular expression, often maintain an extensive illegal underside. In the Communist Party, for example, the distinction between public and private personality is not always clear because the more notorious revolutionaries normally compose the national leadership. However, the conspiratorial mission of the party necessitates the maintenance of a considerable network of members not publicly identified as such, who may be counted on to supply leadership or exercise control over key areas of power and influence if the occasion for a Communist takeover should arise. Thus the Communist Party is considerably more than what it appears to be on the surface, and its impact on French life and on the balance of political power in Parliament is probably greater than its visible size would suggest.

By the same token, extreme rightist parties, which tend to rise and fall in response to specific and often unique political issues, have traditionally served as cloaks for clandestine organizations attempting to carry out the objectives of their leadership by direct action. During the interwar years fascist organizations complete with street armies, clandestine headquarters, and ambitious secret strategies for the seizure of power regularly saw their spokesmen legally elected to the National Assemblies. Today, similar arrangements exist, although much less is known about them. They are, by and large, illegal combinations of a few prominent political figures tied to large blocs of supporters and activists, usually organized into veterans' clubs or action committees. The principal focus of these combinations today is the Algerian issue. Some of these groups would go so far as to destroy the Fifth Republic if they could; all are interested in sabotaging official government policy in Algeria, and all have at least a few deputies in the Assembly. Each group has access to a tribune for its propaganda and its leaders enjoy some degree of personal protection by virtue of their Parliamentary immunity.

When the second Algiers uprising took place in January 1960 a handful of deputies from extreme rightist parties had to be forcibly restrained from leaving Paris to join the insurgents in Algiers. The uprising itself was captained by a young deputy, Pierre LaGaillarde, who subsequently was jailed for his actions. But, as if to emphasize the continuity of the movement he represented—concerning which the police have many dossiers but few suspects—LaGaillarde's wife was a month or two later elected to the municipal council of the city of Algiers although her husband languished in a Paris jail.

The more violent political movements on the far Right are almost entirely covert because their activities are almost wholly illegal. They are usually small; they constantly change names and leaders and claim—perhaps spuriously—supporters in both the military and the civil service. Probably the most notorious are the Red Hand, a group about which little is known, but which specializes in violence, extending from sabotage to murder, directed against proponents of Algerian independence, and the OAS (*Organization de l'Armée Secrète*), an Algerian settler group specializing in terroristic bombing, which supported the army mutiny of April 1961.

The Principal Political Parties

If there is great confusion and flux in the French party system, it is nevertheless true that a great majority of French voters express themselves through more or less traditional parties. Many parties come and go, but a few large ones survive adversities over decades. Occasionally some shattering national experience, such as the coup in Algiers that brought de Gaulle to power, or the *Résistance,* in World War II, throws up a new movement which may come to take its place alongside the regulars. At the moment there are six major parties represented in the National Assembly, a few fragmentary groups with a handful of deputies, and countless local formations with slim hopes of achieving national standing. Of the principal parties, four have long histories in French politics, and one other has enjoyed a vigorous life since World War II. Generally speaking, the major parties represent classical strands in French political thought. The most enduring is, as already noted, the Republican strand, represented in theory, if not always in practice, by the Radicals, or Radical Socialists as they were originally called. Next in line are the Socialists, who can and do claim a political existence predating the spread of Marxist influence in France. The Communists, who split off from the Socialists following World War I, are institutionally younger, but identify themselves with the *sans culottes* of the original revolution. The Independents currently hold down the position of the classical Right—no longer anti-republican, simply conservative and nominally favorable to the church, business interests, and the peasantry. The names of the traditional Right parties have changed from the Third to the Fifth Republics but the principles and the interests involved have remained the same. Even the *Résistance*-born Catholic MRP party had a small forerunner with a few deputies in the parliaments of the Third Republic. At present only the Gaullist party (UNR) is a newcomer to the French political stage. Some pundits claim that even it is merely a throwback to the party of the Bonapartists who crowded the aisles of the first Assemblies of the Third Republic, and then died away at the turn of the century.

The Communist Party

The Communist Party (*Parti Communiste Français*) is fond of applying to itself Lenin's old maxim: "The Communist Party is not a party like the others." In the 1960s this is less true than it was even a few years ago, but nevertheless the party is still unique. It consistently has obtained one-fifth to one-quarter of the popular vote since World War II, and yet its leadership has openly claimed the Soviet Union as its fatherland. A revolutionary force in a modern and sophisticated society, it has drawn to its inner circle some of France's leading intellectuals, many of her most effective labor leaders, as well as a goodly scattering of bureaucratic party hacks. The basic difference between the Communist Party and other political movements in France lies in the fact that it has an ideological and psychological force not found elsewhere. Although the leadership image of President de Gaulle is a powerful and compelling element behind the UNR, the relationship of an average UNR rank and file member to either the general or his party is almost captious compared to the rapport between the average militant Communist and his party. Moreover, the ties between party and militant, between local cell and national headquarters are not only strong, but have been sanctified by the official philosophers of the movement to the point where organizational technique is an integral part of ideology. These are the substantial points which make for the party's distinctiveness.

Discipline is the primary element binding the rank and file member to the Communist Party. Political analysts have offered numerous explanations of the phenomenon of a French party successfully instilling a sense of discipline in its membership, though the French are notoriously individualistic and independent-minded. One theory holds that the party supplies a need which many Frenchmen feel their society does not give them: a sense of direction, a guideline which they can follow without questioning and without doubts. Certainly for many Frenchmen the demand made on them from their earliest years "to reason" is an exhausting obligation. The pseudo-intellectual atmosphere of party functions satisfies the Frenchman's pride by suggesting that he has not given up the struggle for truth. Meanwhile the party conveniently points the path, supplies the leadership and, if necessary, calms all doubts. Another explanation often heard is that the French working class is in fact alienated from the rest of society by the workings of France's narrowly limited, family-capitalized economy. Hence the worker, who views himself as exploited and abandoned, seeks representation in the party which is also alien to the society, whose purpose is to destroy the existing social order, and which glories in its own distinctiveness from all other political forces. Although this picture of the French working class and of the French economy is rapidly becoming less and less valid, it retains its force, because the last myth the traditionalist-minded Frenchman of all classes will give up is the self-pitying image of himself. The party furthermore works day and night to perpetuate this image, and consistently describes the current workings of the French economy as directly contributing to the absolute impoverishment of the masses when the standard of living of the French working class is clearly rising in relation to other classes.

More satisfactory explanations for the party's success in a land of extreme individualists derive from very practical attributes which a small core of the faithful have worked hard to cultivate. For one thing the party—no matter what its motives—did an extraordinary job during the *Résistance* period in World War II. The heroic exploits of Communist martyrs were given wide circulation by professional party propagandists, often to the point where *Résistants* of different political faiths but of equal zeal were overlooked or vilified. The Communists fastened to themselves the label, "party of the martyrs," and could produce the names of thousands of exportees and firing squad victims to make the label stick. When the war ended, Communists moved swiftly to take advantage of chaotic political conditions to provide in many localities the first semblance of order and administration. Through these and many similar actions the party staked out its claim to a major position in French postwar life. The provisional chief of the first postwar government, General de Gaulle, recognized this claim by awarding party leaders three cabinet posts, from which vantage the party colonized large sections of the public service. Although much of the effort undertaken by the party during the *Résistance* has since been vitiated by a long period in political isolation and by government purges of the administration, the party has had an enormous impact throughout the land.

Another attribute of immeasurable importance is the devoted and skillful use of organization employed by a small percentage of dedicated leaders at all levels. The Communists early learned the truth of the political maxim that nothing succeeds like service. Hence, they are prepared to provide their followings with every possible form of personal assistance. In a country not overly given to mutual assistance societies the Communist Party frequently fills the role of welfare headquarters, youth center, pressure group for working class legislation, and employment bureau. Party militants are quick to offer leadership for the drearier tasks involved in local government or in trade union direction. In brief, the party makes a specialty of its indispensability. To a certain extent, this passion for active service tends to produce a certain artificiality in party affairs and in the personal conduct of prominent leaders. Many Frenchmen today find the parade of familiar Communist faces tiresomely passing from one frenzied task to another a bit oppressive, but many others, even those who never associate themselves with the formal machinery, grudgingly respect the apparently boundless energy with which party members conduct their business and which they bring to the task of organizing the party's services to the general public.

Attempts to trace the sources of Communist Party strength in France usually break down early. To be sure there is general agreement—and considerable statistical evidence—concerning the party's strength among organized industrial workers. Not only do the Communists control the largest and most powerful of the three principal unions in France, the *Confédération Générale du Travail,* but Communists often hold a majority of seats on the municipal councils of the industrial suburbs where large numbers of workers make their homes. Paris itself is almost completely surrounded by such towns, which are really extensions of the city proper. This ring of Communist communities has been traditionally called the Red Belt of Paris, because here for generations the inhabitants have voted for the most Left parties, whether Republican a century ago, Socialist before World War II, or Communist thereafter. Significantly, some of these large, ugly urban suburbs have changed little in a hundred years, the housing facilities least of all—a fact that may explain the tradition of leftist voting patterns better than anything else. The more wretched farming areas—especially in the southeast of France—also have large concentrations of Communist voters, as do the bigger port cities in a country where the sea is of prime importance. Intellectuals, journalists, engineers, doctors are represented in the party. In fact it has some strength in all sections of the populace and in all but a few geographic areas.

Generalizations about the appeal of the party are dangerous. We can say, however, that to some it is useful as a vehicle of protest against real or fancied political injustices. To others, especially the lowest-paid workers and the poorest peasants, it is a powerful and effective friend in an otherwise difficult world. To the relatively prosperous working class elite, in the metal and automobile trades for example, the party may represent many things: the most efficient force in a strong union which fights to maintain the exclusiveness of the highest skill classifications in an industry, or the traditional party of grandfather, father, and son. To a few the party may have no special personal meaning except insofar as it has succeeded in fostering the illusion that it is the wave of the future, and hence should be followed for purely selfish reasons.

Clearly the motivations for Communist Party membership discussed above do not constitute an exhaustive list. However, they do suggest that a good percentage of the party membership may faithfully purchase cards for reasons which have little to do with ideology. The exact division of those who believe in the party doctrines and dogma and those who find voting for the party useful for any one of a variety of personal and non-ideological reasons cannot, of course, ever be determined. However, the gap between 4,500,000 voters who normally support the party and the roughly 500,000 card holders who pay at least a portion of their dues annually is a significant index. The ratio between the total number of readers of Communist newspapers and voters is about the same, although the number of faithful interested in the daily twists and turns of the line by consulting either *L'Humanité* or one of the provincial dailies has been declining steadily since World War II. Life for the party activist or *militant* is too demanding for most men. Moreover, in a party the size of the PCF, advancement from the lowest organizational unit, the cell, through section and departmental federation, up to the national organs of central committee and ultimately the political bureau is not only slow, but more often than not reserved for those with some talent for theoretical exposition or oratorical skill.

Despite the dedication of Communist cadres in recent years, the celebrated discipline of the party over its troops has been less than perfect. It is no longer possible for the *grands chefs* of the party—some of whom have been members of the political bureau for over twenty years—to summon thousands of the faithful to political demonstrations or protest marches. The party is in fact in deep organizational troubles. Partly it is a financial crisis. For years the party subsisted on the salaries of its deputies in the National Assembly which were turned in to the party treasurer each month. But after the 1958 election, when the Communist representation was reduced from 180 deputies to ten by the working of the new electoral law, the party treasury lost its best source of revenue. Donations from the rank and file have by no means compensated for this loss, and consequently many party functions and services have been curtailed and several party newspapers suspended. And if the Communists are suffering from a shortage of funds, they are also reaping the bitter harvest of over a decade in opposition. The party has become bureaucratized, its leadership immobilized, its slogans unchanging. In short, there is no new blood in the party, and little chance that there will be any under present conditions. Some of the dynamism on which a revolutionary movement depends is gone; the *malaise* of the party's leadership is inevitably felt throughout the lower echelons.

However, if the party is in a deep trough at the moment, it is not despairing. The search for recruits continues, focused at the moment on the not alogether receptive outcast group of Algerians working in metropolitan France. Curiously, the party cannot afford to overemphasize its criticisms of the generally unpopular Algerian war, nor to make too open an appeal to the Moslems. France's 400,000 resident Algerians are regarded with considerable hostility by the French-born industrial workers who form the party's popular base. Nevertheless, the party remains a formidable presence in the politics of the Fifth Republic. The Communists are in fact encouraged by the opportunities they see in exploiting the misgivings roused in many Frenchmen by what are regarded as the authoritarian tendencies of the de Gaulle regime. They are busy trying to discredit de Gaulle by identifying him with traditional forces of conservatism, by debunking austerity and anti-inflation measures, and above everything else they are seeking political allies with whom they can reconstitute "the unity of the left in the common defense against the return of fascism to France." In the present political atmosphere of diminishing parliamentary influence and continuing tensions over the Algerian war, this is by no means an impotent appeal.

The Socialist Party

Just to the Right of the Communists in the spectrum of French politics (and in the National Assembly) sit the Socialists (*Section Française de l'Internationale Ouvrière*), or the SFIO, as the party is known for short. With about half the popular support enjoyed by the Communists, the Socialists have nearly three times as many elected deputies, but they are a declining political force in France. Encumbered by memories of the past and doctrines that were devised for another era, the Socialists give the impression of being a little old-fashioned. Fittingly, the party's members are on average older than those of most. Party functions have the distinctive atmosphere of old men nostalgically gathering to discuss the great moments of their youth—old men who tend to be annoyed by more lively spirits among them impolitely insisting on new ideas.

It is impossible to understand what makes a Socialist Party member, or even a Socialist voter, tick without looking backward to the turn of the century. In 1900 the party, with a pocket of deputies in the Assembly and a proportionately much larger following scattered in industrial regions throughout the country, was deeply embroiled in the heady passions of the Dreyfus affair. The position of two Socialist leaders on the question of Dreyfus' guilt or innocence symbolizes the two contrasting strains which had characterized the party for some time, did then, and to a certain extent still do. Jules Guesde, who was the principal spokesman of Karl Marx in France, denounced the Dreyfus affair as an artificial struggle "between rival bourgeois factions" and urged the workers to ignore it. However, Jean Jaurès, the most dramatic name in the history of the party, stung by the revelations of Zola and other spokesmen of the radical Left, broke ranks to declare for the Dreyfusards in the name of humanity and individual dignity and in opposition to the "clericals, aristocrats, and militarists." Significantly, Jaurès went on to become the parliamentary leader of the party, and to drive it towards pacifism on the eve of World War I. He died of an assassin's bullet on the day before the war broke out, his dreams of preventing the carnage by an international general strike frustrated by the nationalist passions of both German and French workers. Jaurès represented a curious mixture which can still be found in the SFIO today—a blend of purely French humanitarian socialism and Marxism.

Before the first French publication of Marx's writings in the last quarter of the nineteenth century, an impressive history of socialism had already been established in France—much of it utopian and humanitarian, almost all of it colored in one way or another by the very real and heady impact of personal involvement on the barricades of revolution. The Marxist scorn for heretics of a separate and competing dogma that differed from that of the master was never as successfully used in France as elsewhere in Europe. It could not be because the heretics had very often been engaged in true proletarian battles before, and in some cases after, the arrival of Marxist gospel. Even following the Russian Revolution, when the Communists broke away from the old Second International to set up housekeeping on their own, they represented only a minority of the French working class movement, a "Guesdist" and doctrinaire minority, unlike the large majority which retained a faith in the more supple and humanitarian positions of Jaurès. It was in fact the famous "twenty-one demands," formulated by the Soviet Bolshevik Party and presented to a congress of the French Socialist Party as a minimum set of requirements for acceptance into the new Third International, that caused the final break between Socialists and Communists. Slightly less than half of the leaders of the party refused to accept the dictated conditions which included amongst other things: transformation into a party controlled by its executive, agreement to organize clandestinely and to carry on agitation in the army, full support for the U.S.S.R., and the obligation to purge all those who repudiated the conditions. The small band of leaders who refused to swallow these terms found the majority of the rank and file with them, but the leaders never could establish harmony amongst themselves.

Socialism probably reached its peak in France in 1936 when, with the Communists and Radicals, Léon Blum formed the Popular Front government as a defense against the spread of fascism in the country. This coalition soon proved incompatible, however, and collapsed without adequately preparing the country's defenses for World War II. The party was decimated by the Vichy regime (and compromised by a few of its leaders), during the German occupation, but many of its members performed creditably in the *Résistance* and it emerged as a still powerful force when the war ended.

In the postwar period, however, the SFIO never quite regained the status it had once had with the large industrial working class. For one thing, a few of its leaders were touched by the Vichy taint; for another, the agreement to coordinate with the Communists on all matters of "class legislation" quickly broke down. The splitting of the huge national trade union, the CGT, which had only recently been fused together after an earlier wartime schism, was blamed, and correctly so, on the Socialists, who in 1947 balked at the tactics of the (by then) predominantly Communist leadership in the union. Finally, the Socialists were unable to adjust themselves to the new balance of political power in France. They failed to grasp the importance of radical social changes—many of which they had helped to bring about under the Popular Front—changes that were transforming the industrial proletariat by diversifying its interests and even by diluting its strictly proletarian character. A move to change the SFIO to a labor party similar to the British Labour Party was beaten back by the current Secretary General, Guy Mollet. He and his lieutenants, who have been in almost undisputed control of the party machinery ever since, have insisted on preserving the old slogans and doctrines of a revolutionary credo no longer felt in the hearts of the leaders nor shared by its electorate. Paradoxically, because it was necessary to distinguish itself from the Communist Party, the SFIO collaborated with so-called bourgeois parties throughout the postwar period.

It became in fact a party not of the Left but of the Center-Left, supported by civil servants, by some traditional strongholds in the industrial North, and by scattered pockets of rural radicalism and cooperativism in the Toulouse area and in the Southeast. As its public appeal became less consistent with the image it was trying to maintain, membership fell off, and the militants looking behind them for younger aspirants to power found no one waiting in line. They therefore were able to settle down in key spots in the hierarchy or in comfortably safe constituencies. The party's organization, still patterned after the original revolutionary movement of the nineteenth century, resembles that of the Communists, minus cells and clandestine apparatus, and lacking the same measure of discipline imposed from the top. Indeed, by comparison to the Communists, the Socialists conduct their internal business with a fair degree of democracy. However, decisions of the parliamentary group, often reached in consultation with the top organ of the party, the executive committee, are binding on all deputies. Breaches of discipline are fairly rare and severely punished.

To close this hasty look at the Socialists, it is perhaps useful to trace the postwar record of the party in regard to one aspect of national policy, the colonial question. Traditionally, the Socialists have proclaimed their devotion to the usual liberal objectives of ending imperialism, the reduction of military credits, and the equality of all races. However, in the unusual political circumstances of postwar France, the SFIO felt itself obliged to enter centrist governments for fear that, if it did not do so, the antagonism of the Communists on the Left and the Gaullists or Poujadists on the far Right would destroy the republic. Thus the Socialists found themselves in governments that were fighting the Indo-China war, trying to hold on in Tunisia and Morocco, and deeply and desperately engaged in an effort to liquidate the Algerian nationalist rebellion.

In some cases Socialist leaders were active in the elaboration of colonial policy: Marius Moutet in Indo-China, Robert LaCoste and Edmond Naegelen in Algeria were outstanding examples. The gradual capitulation of the Socialists to this state of affairs was, however, climaxed when Guy Mollet on taking office as Prime Minister in 1956 appeared to be on the verge of offering the rebels a liberal settlement. Arriving in Algiers with a strong parliamentary coalition behind him, he was met by egg-throwing European toughs and quickly reversed his field by adopting the hard line of military repression of the Moslem rebels. After that it was only a matter of time before Algerian policy, and to a certain extent all colonial policy, was abandoned to the politicians of the far Right. Ultimately, however, the Socialists paid for this weakness. The persistence of a majority of the party in retaining a hesitant and ambiguous Algerian policy provoked a small band of influential Socialist leaders in 1959 to split away and join other dissidents, who were either refugees from the Communist Party or long-isolated intellectuals who felt the Communists too authoritarian and the SFIO too ineffectual. With such figures as Albert Gazier and later Pierre Mendès-France in the forefront, these men founded the *Parti Socialiste Unifié* (PSU), dedicated to negotiating with the rebels to end the Algerian war, and to collaborating with the Communists if necessary to lead an effective opposition against de Gaulle on economic and constitutional issues. So far the PSU is small; it has no deputies, but it has significance as a taunting political conscience on the Socialists' left.

The Radicals

Probably the most French of all the French parties is not a party at all. Writers on French politics are consistently baffled as to how they should describe the group which for decades held the center of the political stage, has provided more premiers than any other party, and which once (but no longer) claimed the revolutionary Jacobins as their spiritual ancestors. These are the Radical Socialists, who dominated the governments of the Third Republic, but who were bitterly riven by the vote taken in the National Assembly in the tragic summer of 1940 to determine whether the republic should abandon its powers to Marshal Pétain. More than half the Radicals voted to do so and consequently doomed their party to years in the political wilderness. Nonetheless, after the war a remnant of the party returned and produced from thinned ranks scores of premiers and prominent cabinet ministers.

By mid-century the Radicals had begun to take on the characteristics of any political movement that has lost all sense of identity. A process of fragmentation started which is still in full swing. Splits occurred over personalities, following expulsions of important leaders, and even over issues! It is now quite accurate to say that there is no longer a Radical Socialist Party, although among several small groups in the National Assembly loosely gathered under constantly changing titles (at this writing they were calling themselves variously the *Entente Democratique, La Gauche Democratique et Radical Socialiste* and/or *Libertés Democratiques*) there are individual Radical Socialists, and it is as Radical Socialists that the voters think of them, regardless of the etiquettes they have adopted. Perhaps it is appropriate that the Radical Socialists should dissolve into a mere collection of individuals, because for years they symbolized the party of the French average man: republican, outspokenly progressive in debate but cautiously conservative in practice, anti-clerical, and firmly nationalist. Far to the Left in the early days of the Third Republic, the Radical Socialists became increasingly heterogeneous and opportunist as the objectives for which they had originally fought—the deep rooting of republican institutions, aggressive defense of individual liberties, and neutralization of the special privileges of the church—appeared to be fully accepted by the French people. The danger of failing to supplant the political goals achieved with new principles and objectives was brutally revealed in 1940 when many Radical Socialists voted to ditch the republic, thereby forfeiting their liberties and those of their countrymen, and preparing the way for the restoration of a professedly clerical state.

In recent years the Radical Socialists have drawn their strength increasingly from rural areas, where as local notables and village councillors they are strong supporters of crop price supports. There are various shades of Radical Socialists; some on the Left probably yearn to join their ex-colleague Pierre Mendès-France in the truly radical PSU, some on the Right, like André Morice, are counted among the "ultras" on the Algerian question. A larger number are primarily concerned with local issues and, at least until the powerful election swing to the Right in 1958, with preserving their crucial position in the Center of the Assembly from which they were easily available to fill ministerial chairs. As befits them, the Radical Socialists tolerate almost no party discipline and, although their party has a national organization and a machinery of sorts, effective power is exercised by isolated individuals who control large personal followings and command some national prominence.

The MRP

One major French party owes its birth to a great historical event, the *Résistance*. The *Mouvement Républicain Populaire* (MRP)—the only admittedly Catholic party in France—sprang not only to life, but even to overblown maturity in the first election that followed the Liberation, when it became one of *les trois grands* which monopolized French governments for several years thereafter. Originating as a party of the Left and a champion of the currents of social reform that animated the *Résistance,* the MRP has since moved steadily toward the Center and, sharply reduced in size and importance, is a somewhat restive partner in de Gaulle's rightist coalition. A more significant aspect of the MRP's place in French history, however, is not that it finally established itself, but that it took so long to do so. The lay republic had become the foundation stone of French democratic politics by the turn of the century. The church was, symbolically at least, a brooding and vengeful force lurking offstage in hopes of recapturing its appropriated estates, its special privileges in community affairs and education, and its important role in political life. Small wonder that when Socialists, Radicals, and even deputies of the Center and moderate Right found themselves incapable of exploiting real political issues in the interwar years, they tilted ferociously at the windmills of the church. As often as not, moreover, the church could be counted on from time to time to spew up obligingly some particularly odious scapegoat—an army officer engaged in fascist activities, or a pious entrepreneur adept at swindle and strike-breaking—who kept the popular image alive. However, while some bishops were dealing with the seamier sides of covert anti-republican activity, the great majority of the Catholic hierarchy in France had long since accepted the inevitable. Most priests were more deeply concerned with accommodation to republicanism than with sabotage. Significantly, a healthy Catholic labor movement had taken root following World War I, and while it did not indulge in the revolutionary phantasies of its non-Catholic rivals, it slowly proved itself a militant and effective fighter for economic benefits and social reform.

It was these elements of Catholicism in France, plus a scattering of widely respected intellectuals and the Catholic Youth Movement, that made up the muscle, blood, and bones of the new party following the Liberation. The record of Catholics in the *Résistance* was stirring enough to make the average Frenchman overlook the fact that some prominent members of the hierarchy had been openly *"Pétainist"* in the first years of the occupation, and that an early Vichy minister of education had attempted to put public schools under the tutelage of the church. Perhaps equally important, the political parties which survived the ravages of the war were faced with a task of national reconstruction so great that they accepted the help of any movements not specifically tainted with collaboration. Thus the leaders of the MRP were proving themselves in responsible positions of authority in the provisional government before they had been subjected to the first electoral tests. Finally, the MRP owed its original success to the fact that the traditional parties of the Right were in complete disarray following the Liberation, and normally conservative voters with no place else to go swamped the lists of the party in the belief that self-styled Catholics of the Left would be less objectionable than non-Catholics of the Left. In subsequent years when the rightist parties re-emerged, the popular support of the MRP dropped. However, the party apparatus was never completely captured by the conservatives, although its character no longer reflects the reforming and humanitarian zeal of the immediate postwar period.

Indeed, the MRP became the essential fixture of almost all postwar governments—frequently the most moderate member of Center-Left coalitions and occasionally the most progressive partner in Center-Right coalitions. In this strategic position it could and did demand important ministerial posts and on several occasions the premiership. For almost a decade French foreign affairs were directed by two MRP foreign ministers, Georges Bidault and Robert Schuman. Other leaders were prominent in ministries concerned with social affairs, labor, and reconstruction —only the ministry of education was by tacit agreement of the republican parties denied to Catholic statesmen. The party, although generally supported throughout the country, fares best in predominantly rural areas and has its largest battalions in the traditionally clerical regions of Brittany and Alsace-Lorraine. The party's doctrines are, as we have said, progressive in economic and social matters but not radical, paternalist but not authoritarian. In foreign policy Robert Schuman was an early and enthusiastic champion of European integration, but the party's record on colonial issues, especially Algeria, is somewhat ambiguous. Perhaps symbolically, the last premier of the Fourth Republic, Pierre Pflimlin, a somewhat colorless MRP politician, was the target of bitter "ultra" demonstrations in Algeria which precipitated the downfall of the republic when the "ultras" became suspicious that he would negotiate with the rebel movement. One of his most formidable detractors was Georges Bidault, by then himself an "ultra." Bidault now heads a tiny breakaway fraction of the MRP of no particular consequence that proclaims itself opposed to any compromise on the Algerian question.

The UNR

The largest party in France is *La Union pour la Nouvelle République* (UNR), which most refer to simply as "de Gaulle's party," although he has refused to become a member of it, preferring to believe that he belongs to all Frenchmen. The UNR is more an amalgam of groups and individuals who have associated themselves with the general at various occasions in the years since World War II than it is a homogeneous political force. Although there is much talk of Gaullism as a political faith in France, few UNR members would agree on its basic principles; fewer still would be able to summarize the platform of the party or distinguish which parts of it are elaborations of de Gaulle's own beliefs and which are simply restatements of conservative principles normally voiced by rightist parties. Attached to de Gaulle are numerous organizations that have called for changes of various kinds in French institutions and policies, and which accept the general not necessarily as the best spokesman of their interests but as the man most likely to bring about change. On the other hand, there are probably as many Gaullists who dislike the implications of radical change in the president's control of the state, but are strongly attracted by de Gaulle's leadership qualities. Thus, it is possible for an essentially conservative French military officer to belligerently oppose the government's Algerian policies, which are devised by de Gaulle, but to grudgingly support the administration nevertheless, as necessary for national dignity. By the same token, a voter with Socialist leanings who disagrees completely with de Gaulle's domestic policies, may endorse the general because he believes that the latter may one day solve the Algerian problem when it is clear that no one else can.

To chart the historical course of this curious political phenomenon it is necessary to go back to de Gaulle's lonely efforts to reestablish the French nation during World War II. Some of those who first followed him into exile and contributed, either politically or militarily, to the tasks of building the Free French movement and ultimately reestablishing it on French soil, are still devoted to the General; they retained their confidence in him during his long retirement from public life from 1945 to 1958, and now are occupying key posts in his government or in the UNR. Most of this fragment of the party is primarily concerned with the renewal of national dignity promised by de Gaulle. They rarely question the methods or tactics which may be necessary to achieve "a reinvigoration of national spirit," assuming, probably quite correctly, that any significant changes in French *élan* are more likely to arise from the force of de Gaulle's personality than anything else. This concept of national renewal, and the Frenchmen who are aroused by its promise, probably constitute the most basic elements of Gaullism.

More specific aspects of the elastic set of the UNR's doctrines developed from a series of speeches critical of the Fourth Republic delivered by de Gaulle in the years between 1945 and 1947. By and large the General belittled Parliament, emphasized the need for strong executive institutions, spoke vaguely about the necessity of forming "associations of capital and labor"—which to some listeners evoked suspicions of fascist corporativism—and bluntly condoned the use of government intervention to guide and strengthen the national economy. In 1947 the *Ralliement du Peuple Français* (Rally of the French People) was born to give expression to these ideas; it proclaimed that it was not a political party and that all Frenchmen save the Communists were welcome under the banner of the RPF. Although elected president of the movement, de Gaulle himself stayed aloof. But the leaders of the rally made clear their determination to return the general to Paris. In its first electoral contest—an election for municipal councillors—the RPF won over a third of the seats in municipalities all over France. In 1951 the RPF attracted the votes of millions of traditional conservative voters and placed 120 deputies in the Assembly. However, the elected deputies soon forgot that their movement was not a party, and the Assembly bloc quickly fragmented into rival rightist groups. By 1953 even General de Gaulle had washed his hands of the rally. His retirement seemed more complete than ever. However, under the lead of Jacques Soustelle and Chaban-Delmas, a remnant of the Gaullist movement hung on in the Assembly under the name Social Republicans, growing increasingly critical of the Fourth Republic's inept governments, its foreign policy, and the continual erosion of the French position in Algeria. This was the parliamentary nucleus for today's UNR, but others also took a hand in giving political momentum and cohesion to the scattered groups who opposed the Fourth Republic. The *coup d'état* in Algiers in May 1958, provided the spark for coalition. To the traditional Gaullists came extreme right-wing elements, such as the Republican Convention of Léon Delbecque, who had been in the forefront of extra-legal activities in Algiers. Literally dozens of organizations threw in their lot with the UNR, whose 230 deputies now dominate the first National Assembly of the Fifth Republic.

Thus, the best description of the party at this writing is that it is a motley collection, normally united on the single proposition of loyalty to President de Gaulle. In the first two years of its life, however, the party has lost its earliest militant, Soustelle, plus several other prominent deputies, and contains many other potential dissidents. It is, in essence, a vehicle for the continuation in power of the general. This, however, is its most glaring weakness. Failure in any one of a number of fields —Algerian policy, economic policy—could set in motion dangerously centrifugal tendencies.

Moreover, the longer the party survives the more likely are the potential divisions within it to take concrete shape. The normally conservative supporters of de Gaulle—even those who accept his Algerian policies—may not long be comfortable with his insistence on massive expenditures for a nuclear weapons program or with his strong views on the necessity for reform of the French commercial system. On the other hand, liberals within the UNR, determined not to allow the party to settle down into a comfortable, middle-of-the-road conservatism, have consistently pressed for adoption of progressive platforms, particularly in the social and economic fields. They lose no opportunities to remind the party's leadership, which is generally drawn from among the more conservative deputies, that the movement has always proclaimed itself neither of the Left nor of the Right, and that its future prospects can only be assured by using strong executive institutions and political discipline to effect sweeping social changes. Some admirers of de Gaulle on the moderate Left, who fear that the conservatives' grip on the UNR is too tight, sustain their pressure on the Gaullists from outside the mass party. They are organized into a small political formation of their own, the *Union Démocratique du Travail* (UDT), with the expressed aim of associating de Gaulle's prestige with liberal objectives. So far they have attracted few followers, but they might at some future date—especially if the UNR were to fragment—serve as a focus for the development of a new political movement.

Thus, fragmentation is the gravest peril facing the UNR once the Algerian problem is settled. The tender fabric of party loyalties was dangerously stretched during the Algiers insurrection in January 1960. It will experience continuing internal crises as the political convictions of its pro-French Moslem Algerian Deputies, now numbering about thirty, are tested against the realities of a settlement that may deprive them of effective influence in their home constituencies. Finally, once de Gaulle, himself, has departed, Gaullism, unless it discovers a new political *raison d'être,* risks becoming a latter-day Bonapartism, growing increasingly less meaningful as the shadow of the man who gave the movement unity fades.

The Independents

Logically enough, the largest French party, in terms of popular support, and second only to the UNR in parliamentary representation, calls itself the Independents. Some 132 deputies from many different political origins cling loosely to this label, although at the same time they belong to subgroups within the larger whole, such as the *Parti Paysan d'Union Sociale* (Peasants' Party) or the *Républicains Indépendents* (Independent Republicans). In reality the Independents, no matter what their particular ancestry, are the collective expression of traditional conservatism in France. Powerful in the Third Republic, but divided among themselves into several distinct parties, they went into temporary eclipse as a political force after World War II. Many right-wing deputies were forever excluded from French political life for collaboration with the occupier, or suspicion of collaboration. Others, who either avoided being tarred by the collaborationist brush or were legally "rehabilitated," generally refrained from entering active public life until the political climate had become more receptive to their return. Indeed it was not until 1951 that the traditional Right revived fully as a significant political force in France, and when it did it was in direct competition with the more dynamic and less tarnished RPF, forerunner of the UNR.

But the roots of conservatism are deep in France, and the various right-wing parties which solidified their positions in 1951 soon absorbed much of the RPF strength as well as a number of the rally's deputies. Businessmen of all sizes and the most prosperous peasants have always provided the basic following of the conservative parties. With some minor variation between them, they ran on common platforms calling for freedom from government controls—coupled with positive state financial assistance and subsidies—a strong upper legislative house to minimize radical tendencies in the Assembly, a generally aggressive colonial policy, and a vigorous nationalist foreign policy. The Independents claimed respected leaders, too—among them Paul Reynaud, the last premier of the Third Republic, and Antoine Pinay, who became de Gaulle's first minister of finance. Today, their various fractions are more consolidated than in the past. They form an integral part of the de Gaulle-Debré coalition, giving the government in all its parts a heavily conservative cast, thus neutralizing some of the more uninhibited reformist tendencies on the left of the UNR. Some of the wilder "ultras" on the Algerian question are found on the benches of the Independents, while at the same time the party contains men, such as Pinay, who feel that retention of Algeria is probably not worth the economic drain on France. Fortunately the organization of the party is so loose that it can easily contain these disparate elements. For the most part each deputy or local official running on the Independent ticket maintains his own local apparatus, although a convention of members is held once a year, and the parliamentary representatives do subject themselves to a minimum degree of discipline on certain selected issues. Discipline is not, however, an overwhelmingly important consideration for a party whose members are primarily tied together by shared views on bread and butter issues.

The fate of seventy deputies from Algeria, who were originally elected to the Assembly in 1958, remains unclear. The great majority at first seated themselves between the UNR and the Independents and adopted the name Group for the Unity of the Republic. Basically reactionary, most of these deputies were wholly concerned with the notion that Algeria must remain part of France. After his expulsion from the UNR Jacques Soustelle attempted to assert his leadership over the group, but its numbers and influence have diminished as individual deputies dropped away to join the UNR, the Independents, or retire into complete isolation. Soustelle's group now contains almost as many European extremist deputies as Moslems.

Conclusions

The emphasis in this chapter on the historical origins and derivations of French parties perhaps may seem out of place in a study of Western Europe's newest government. Nevertheless, the fact remains that the new institutions of France are by and large being tested on a people who vote for parties that came to life under very different circumstances. Apart from the UNR and the extremely parochial Group for the Unity of the Republic, all the other political formations predate the Fifth Republic, if not the Fourth. For this reason the UNR tends to stand alone, even from its formal partners within the coalition, or rather it is isolated by the other parties as a symbol of that which is new, strange, and in some respects threatening. For there are few politicians who can forget or forgive the fact that de Gaulle and the UNR rode to power by strongly criticizing the existing party system and by suggesting that the UNR was not really a party in the old sense, but a political meeting place for Frenchmen of Right and Left alike. This somewhat pretentious notion jarred the traditional political leaders who resented the Gaullists' constant taunt that they were to blame for French weakness.

Following the 1958 election, when less than 25 per cent of the deputies from the last Assembly of the Fourth Republic were reelected, many French politicians began to fear that the people shared the contempt expressed by the UNR. Nevertheless, a crisis of the traditional parties, anticipated by many and forecast by a few, has not yet come. There have been cracks in the solid front of the Socialists, and the Catholics are now for all intents and purposes two parties, but these strains are still by no means serious.

The political institutions have been revolutionized, the economy has undergone drastic changes, even the basic political issues of French life are no longer what they were a scant ten years ago, although many old problems remain unresolved. Yet the parties remain essentially unaffected by these developments. A partial explanation can be found in the natural reluctance of man to throw off the old clothes to which he is accustomed—especially when all else around him is changing. But this is probably not a satisfactory answer. More important is the highly tentative way in which many Frenchmen regard the Fifth Republic. This is not to say that de Gaulle's accession to power and even the changes he has brought about are not popular with the French, but rather that on the whole the "Great Experiment" is still regarded with a mixture of incredulity, some satisfaction, and a healthy dose of cynicism. The general is thought of not altogether as an aberration, but at least as unique. Beyond him lies the probability of a return to leaders of a lesser breed, in short the familiar faces of "the system." Moreover, the average Frenchman, no matter what his personal feelings toward de Gaulle, is well aware that he took office with an embarrassing set of legacies, notably the Algerian problem and the unruly behavior of the military, which if they are not somehow resolved, could once again lead France into new political adventures. Therefore, it is only prudent for the Frenchman to keep a reserve of faith in his time-honored political party, no matter what the political circumstances. If he is a Socialist, the party will protect his paycheck; if he is a Radical, it will insure against the encroachments of the church; and if he is an Independent, it will take care that the government purchases his excess alcohol production at satisfactory prices. Finally, then, it must be concluded that the future of the parties, like so many other things in France, depends on the success or failure of de Gaulle. If his regime becomes firmly planted, the traditional parties will slowly adapt to the new conditions; if not, they will remain what they are today, essentially conservative or inhibiting forces in a fluid political situation.

7 - Government and the Economy

The peculiar French compulsion to interpret human and natural phenomena in terms of an all-embracing philosophy is not consistently applied to the economy. To be sure, many political leaders have sought to impose their systems of thought on the economic process of the nation, but the job has been too great for normally short-lived French administrations. Premiers and ministers of France, coming and going with dizzy speed, have left only fleeting imprints on the basic shape of the economy as it was when France entered the twentieth century. Thus the present situation is one in which many men with varying philosophies have had a hand; a whole network of controls, regulations and institutions has grown up at different points in French history, one element inspired by a conservative economic thinker, another by what the French insist on calling a *dirigiste* (or planner), still another by an out-and-out Marxist. In many ways the government's relation to the economy is not dissimilar to that found in the United States where remnants of *laissez faire* Hooverism exist side by side with New Dealism, self-regulated business, or pure economic opportunism.

As there are no rules guiding the development of the government's role in the economy, there is no logical pattern of government-sponsored social services that implements a given social philosophy. Social security exists in some areas but not in others. Family allowances are available to all, but to a considerable degree their purpose has been distorted and in some cases they virtually supplant wages as the primary form of personal income. The government is an active promoter and regulator in a number of minor economic sectors; in many important ones it is entirely absent.

This curious quality of the French government's role in controlling or guiding the economy and providing welfare for its citizens is essentially a consequence of the weakness and instability of political traditions. Not only have transitory governments embarked on ambitious economic and social programs only to be overturned in a few months by another with different objectives, but these same weak governments have been easy prey for a host of competing special interest groups seeking protection or benefits from a benevolent state. Moreover, most governments in the twentieth century, at least, have been obliged to take into account the fact that the French economy itself is somewhat of a paradox. It contains some of the most dynamic and progressive large industries in Western Europe, and yet it is still strongly influenced by the psychology of the small, inefficient producer and his far more numerous commercial counterparts.

The development of the country is also quite uneven, large areas, especially in Brittany and the Southwest, lagging far behind the rest of the nation in terms of economic vitality, economic growth and living standards. French soil is probably the richest in Europe, arable land plentiful, but the poor organization of agricultural production and distribution has made French food prices the highest on the continent, and on occasion has necessitated the importing of foodstuffs. Sound historical explanations exist for many of these weaknesses, gaps and paradoxes in the French economic structure. We cannot here be concerned with these reasons, but we must recognize they are so important to the French economic scene that they preoccupy all French planners and economists. The political imperatives of caring first for the small farmer, or adjusting tax rates so that they do not overburden the poorest section of the country—these problems absorb energies that might otherwise be expended in the creation of a truly modern society.

The State as Planner

Ambitious efforts have been made from time to time to adopt logical programs of economic and social action that would chart new courses for the French economy. These have been essentially of two types: (1) sweeping political programs so all-inclusive as to amount to complete charters of social-economic reform; and (2) national economic plans, largely devoid of political connotations, that have had as ends in themselves the expansion and strengthening of the economy. The most explosive and dramatic example of the first type was the Popular Front program of 1936, a massive assault on economic institutions which had for decades preserved a hopelessly conservative capitalism against persistent social outcries and had survived even the deteriorating effects of the Great Depression. The Popular Front program, compounded from the platforms of the tripartite (Radical, Socialist, Communist) Front and the so-called "Plan" of the labor unions, like any political amalgam was framed to please many tastes. It was by no means comprehensive or integrated one part to another. However, by extending the responsibility of the government more deeply than ever before into the economy, it irrevocably changed the face of French business. Moreover, for all its faults the Popular Front in one year successfully achieved most of its goals: nationalization of the Bank of France and armament industries; imposition of a sharply graduated income tax; the establishment of a National Wheat Board to provide the government with a lever for controlling crop production and guaranteeing minimum incomes for the producers; the institutionalization of a government-protected system of collective bargaining, and the beginning of a system of compulsory arbitration of labor disputes. Perhaps it is too generous to fix the label "planning" on this mixed bag of economic reforms. Taken singly, each of the measures, although until then considered highly controversial, was sorely needed in France at the time and would have been welcome for its own sake. In combination, they raised the living standards of the peasants and increased the political strength of the industrial working class, without radically altering the economy. However, the opportunity to test the new levers of national economic control won by the Popular Front was short-lived as war clouds gathered in Europe and the leaders of all parties quickly became preoccupied with tooling up defense industries.

The next leap forward in the extension of government authority in the social and economic fields came as a result of the profound soul-searching experienced by the French during their years of resistance to the German occupier. The National Council of the Resistance, a small governing committee of representatives from all the major clandestine *Résistance* organizations, produced in March 1944 a blueprint for France's future which called for the nationalization of primary resources and energy, state direction of banks and insurance, elimination of trusts in private business, and the participation of labor in industrial management. These were radical aims indeed which could have paved the way for a planned economy, if fully implemented. However, in the warm flush of national unity occasioned by the hope of national regeneration, the Charter of the Resistance was accepted by most political elements in France, and even endorsed by such well-known conservatives as General de Gaulle.

Following the Liberation the planks of the Charter were put high on the agenda of the Provisional Government. Most of the nationalization measures were quickly enacted; less fruitful efforts were made to meet the other demands by a leftist-dominated legislature which acted out of a sense that it was more necessary to correct social evils and injustices of the past than to detail or dovetail the requirements of the future. The two historic phases of the Popular Front period and the Resistance Charter cannot simply be dismissed as politically opportune adjustments by which the workers and *résistants* were dissuaded from taking what they regarded as their share by direct, violent means. The reforms springing from both periods were essential to the health of the French economy and permitted it to move ahead in the postwar years on a basis competitive with its European neighbors.

The necessity for regularizing formal and systematic economic planning that would carry on despite changes in political administration was finally recognized after World War II with the creation of the *Commissariat Général au Plan.* The commissariat, brain child of the vigorous ex-civil servant Jean Monnet, who later was to contribute so much to European integration, was given the mission not only of reconstructing the war-torn French economy, but of determining which sectors of the economy required modernization or strengthening. In the early postwar period when government economic controls were still stringent, it was possible to implement the decisions of the planners. Eight basic sectors were selected for special attention in the first five year plan (1947–1952): coal, electricity, steel, cement, farm machinery, transportation, fertilizers, and fuel. Control of investment by the government was facilitated in some of these primary fields because they had long been operated by the state (transportation), or had been recently nationalized (coal, electricity). Private investment was guided by investment commissions within the commissariat, and occasionally provided directly from government funds through a National Modernization and Equipment Fund which was generously supported by American financial assistance through the European Recovery Program. The strong impetus given to the recovery and modernization of the French economy by the first plan—whose life was extended an additional two years—was supplemented by the work of the second or Hirsch

Plan, which concentrated on secondary industries, housing, and the strengthening of the economies of the overseas territories.

A glance at current planning demonstrates that emphasis is now on elimination of obstacles to the general expansion of the economy, and the strengthening of France's fiscal position, rather than on the shoring up or modernization of primary elements in the economic picture. The planners are now concerning themselves with such problems as the supply of teachers, water transport, improving the standards of the pharmaceutical profession, etc. As emphasis in planning is shifted from the purely economic to those questions with social and political implications, it seems probable that the plan will come to have less force and significance in the society. Certainly planning will be exposed to more political sniping and criticism from the Assembly. The days when the basic contours of the plan were accepted almost without comment by the Assembly are probably passed. Nevertheless, it is also true that the centralized machinery of the Fifth Republic provides a better vehicle for state economic planning than did the Fourth: a future administration, armed with the strong precedents of both the Monnet and Hirsch periods behind it, could, if it so chooses, swing the immense power of the government with great firmness into a commanding position in the mainstream of the economy.

Relations between the State and Business

Any understanding of the complex and often Byzantine relations between the French state and the business world must begin with the recognition of a cold historical fact: the general pattern of relations was instituted under governments of the Third and Fourth Republics, all more or less prey to the demands and pressures of numerous industrial, commercial and other special interests. Whatever degree of independence from these pressures the Fifth Republic enjoys or will enjoy in the future, it is nevertheless encumbered—and is likely to remain so for some time to come—with inescapable habits and political obligations deriving from the uneven development of the French economy. Only a truly revolutionary government, indifferent to the human consequences of sweeping reversals of traditional practices, could hope to eliminate fully the influence of business on the processes of government. In this sense, at least, the de Gaulle regime has not proved revolutionary. Nevertheless it may be expected to move gradually toward the alteration of the power relations in the state-business nexus so that the former can act more positively and independently and less in response to transitory economic pressures.

The primary tools by which the French government controls business are: public investment (both in the nationalized areas of the economy and in guiding private investment into officially approved channels by exercise of the planning machinery), price control and taxation. These areas are normal ones for action by modern industrial states, and it should be remembered that in France, unlike the United States, little natural prejudice exists against the active and often aggressive state manipulation of these levers to produce desired economic results. Depending on the economic philosophy of any given administration, liberality in the economy can either be enhanced or weakened simply by restricting or increasing the government's role. Almost always this can be done through simple administrative action, although in the two most sensitive spheres of price controls and taxes, the pressures on the Ministry of Finance, where the decisions are made, frequently come first from the legislature. If the Fifth Republic differs significantly from its predecessors in this regard, it is in the removal of finance ministers from exposure to direct and oppressive bullying tactics by the Assembly spokesmen of special economic interests.

Subsidies, preferential rates for certain businesses in government-operated transportation, and selective export licensing are a few of the more obvious mechanisms by which the government indirectly achieves the objectives of its overall economic policies. And of these only the first is susceptible in any significant degree to abuse by powerful business interests. In the field of taxation, however, the government has considerably less leverage over business, because taxes are established uniformly and normally require legislative approval. In addition to taxes on corporation incomes, a production tax on each stage of the extractive or fabricating process is levied on a percentage of the successive value added. There are also commercial taxes on every transfer of goods short of the purely retail level. While business taxes are high in total volume, they are not necessarily discriminatory or arbitrary. Nevertheless, the existence of high tax rates does tend to operate to the disadvantage of certain types of business, especially those that are large or of a complex, highly technical nature.

However, in a mixed economy, such as the French, distinctions between discriminatory and nondiscriminatory taxes have a tendency to get blurred. So many of the basic economic decisions of the society can be made directly in the Ministry of Finance or in the office of the state-operated Bank of France, that as often as not inequities in the overall system can be removed by special exemptions. Existence of a large number of nationalized industries and services simplifies the task of the government economists. By effectively controlling the pricing policies and in some cases managing such primary sectors as coal, rail and water transportation, the armament industry, and the national credit structure, by dominating the automobile industry through ownership of Renault, and by participating in the operation of a number of other basic fields such as petroleum through partial ownership arrangements, the government can and does have an immediate, if indirect, influence on almost all aspects of the economy.

The nationalized industries function for the most part under the nominal control of public boards on which representatives of labor, the managerial apparatus, and the consumers or clientele of the enterprise in question are seated. In practice, however, the government has retained a strong hand through its authority to appoint the general managers, whose powers have slowly increased at the expense of the public boards. More and more basic policy is determined by the ministries under whose overall guidance the nationalized industries fall—and in some cases by inter-ministerial committees.

Thus politics is very much a part of business, or at least of big business. The powers of government in the economy have grown in recent years to the point where they are ponderous. Any incoming premier has at his fingertips a vast number of controls and financial instrumentalities which, if he chooses to use them, can significantly affect the economic life of France. However, because few politicians are equipped with the highly technical skills necessary to manipulate these controls and instruments toward other than immediate, short-range objectives, two general consequences result. Either economic decisions are made under the spur of political considerations, or the decisions are taken by permanent bureaucrats tucked away deep within the ministries and unhampered by the restraints of political responsibility. The rising importance of anonymous technocrats in the Fifth Republic is another aspect of the executive's steady retreat from public responsiveness and legislative accountability.

The Government and Agriculture

Traditionally in France the government has concerned itself with the agricultural problem—an issue that in one aspect or another almost yearly embroils the legislature and the cabinet in bitter political debate. Agriculture has always had a special place in French life, perhaps because, as we noted in Chapter 2, it is spread throughout the length and breadth of the nation. Even the term "peasant" has an emotional connotation for most Frenchmen; in no other country in the world does food play such an important part in the national culture; every Frenchman fancies himself something of an expert in the quality of foodstuffs and of viniculture. Thus, it is not surprising that the agricultural problem is charged with political dynamite. Every politician must have a solution to the problem and every administration must deal with it sooner or later. In actual fact all modern administrations have dabbled in the fields of marketing control and price subsidization and a few have even dared venture into the far more controversial and primary areas of land ownership and inheritance.

The question of size and ownership of individual farms is in France, as everywhere else in the world, the critical one for agriculture. However, in France small farming is not only a national institution, it is almost a subject of national reverence, not unlike the family farm in the national mythology of the United States. What is probably the largest and most vociferous, if not the most effective, pressure group in the nation is the *Fédération Nationale des Syndicats d'Exploitants Agricoles*. The FNSEA, as it is called, is dedicated to supporting by direct and indirect methods its philosophy that "family agriculture is the base of the whole French economy." In this effort it has secured the active cooperation of countless deputies, most of the principal parties, and probably a good slice of the public at large.

The political strength of the small farmer has militated against the rationalization of French agriculture as a whole and has slowed the introduction of progressive techniques in farm production and distribution. Nevertheless valiant efforts have repeatedly been made with varying success by many governments anxious to remove this notorious bottleneck in the French economy. Legislation has attacked but never solved the problem of separated strip farming whereby one peasant may work as many as fifteen or twenty uneconomic disconnected parcels of land, and the far more complex difficulty of inheritance patterns which have traditionally resulted in one farm's passing by division to all the direct heirs of a deceased owner. Similarly, government credit institutions (the *Caisses Nationales de Crédit Agricole*) have been made available to facilitate the farmer's purchase of larger holdings or for improvement and modernization of plant. Not surprisingly the first plan of the *Commissariat au Plan* gave primary attention to the modernization of farming and funneled a high proportion of its funds to the purchase of machinery and the development of fertilizers. Government-sponsored extension services have also been increased in rural areas, although the distrust of the average peasant for the "government man" 's advice has tended to minimize the impact of this service.

For every positive government step taken to improve the methods and techniques of French farming and to reduce the inhibiting conservative influence of the marginal family farm, there are dozens of government subsidies and other props in operation which make the survival of the small farm possible and which do nothing to discourage the overproduction of crops that cannot be sold at a profit, but continue to be produced out of habit, tradition, or ignorance. Moreover, special privileges are even accorded particular regions, as in the case of the government's traditional purchasing of excess wine produced in Algeria, and the government's fixing of commodity price differentials in several distinct areas of metropolitan France.

Despite the enormous strength and prestige of the de Gaulle government at its accession to power and the obvious zest with which the Gaullist reformers tackled the problem, there have been few recent changes in the overall pattern of French agriculture. The most significant step was probably that taken to fulfill a number of other and only indirectly related requirements in the fields of improving the commercial system and of urban renewal. This was the effort by the de Gaulle administration to eliminate from the heart of Paris the Central Market, known as *les Halles*. This vast, ancient, sprawling market, partially open air, constitutes the national receiving point for wholesale produce and foodstuffs raised throughout the country. From *les Halles* thousands of distributors transport products daily to and from local markets, often returning them for final retail marketing to provinces where they were originally grown.

The cost of this archaic institution in terms of transportation, spoilage, and middleman charges, all added to the ultimate price paid by the consumer, is incalculable. Nevertheless, the Gaullist offensive against *les Halles* has been blunted by the resistance of the distributors and of the peasant organizations. Some provincial cities have been assisted in the expansion of purely regional markets, but the prestige and continued dominance of *les Halles* remains as a monument to the stubborn French partiality for the family enterprise and the small producer. Indeed a conservatively oriented government, such as de Gaulle's, no matter what its freedom to deal with other issues, is probably least well equipped to act against institutional obstacles to agricultural reform. Because its popular support is derived in great measure from the peasants, the *commerçants,* and other small rural entrepreneurs, and because it appeals for a return to traditional values, it can ill afford to bite the hand that feeds the nation.

Industrial Relations, Collective Bargaining, and Social Security

One of the great ironies of French history is that while the socialist element has played a large and melodramatic role in political developments since the mid-nineteenth century, organized labor has only intermittently been able to assert any significant degree of productive political power. As a consequence labor legislation is uneven at best and there are glaring gaps in the social security system. Labor's political ineffectiveness stems from many things, but the two principal causes can probably be traced to the early character of the trade union movement and the subsequent tendency of trade unionists to divide the labor movement into rival, if not warring, ideological camps. French trade unionism had a chaotic early history and was legally, if not always effectively, outlawed until the last quarter of the nineteenth century. It was virtually wrenched into full life by the aggressive efforts of a handful of anarcho-syndicalists. These spirited pioneers cared little for formal organization and dedicated themselves instead to rallying the workers to prepare themselves for the "coming revolution" which would put an end to capitalism and reestablish society around the primary focus of the workshop or unions. The weapons of the movement were uncompromising and direct: sabotage, violence, and the general strike. Syndicalist theory, such as it was, held that transformation of society would come about sooner or later as the consequence of a general strike whose impact would be so profound throughout the nation that the old capitalist, parliamentary system could not survive.

Possessed of such goals and tactics the French labor movement made little progress in the day-to-day business of social reform and protective labor legislation of the sort already entering the statute books of Germany, Great Britain, and the Scandinavian countries by the turn of the nineteenth century. The Socialist Party attempted to make good these shortcomings prior to World War I, but received little help from scornful revolutionary labor leaders, who cared nothing for the politicians. Inevitably the gap between revolutionary expectations and the hard realities of depressed working class living standards became more and more apparent and painful.

By World War I a few labor leaders (as well as many Socialists) had adopted the infinitely more comfortable—and more immediately rewarding—path of reformism: working for changes in the existing social and economic system through political pressure and legislative action. When Jean Jaurès, the great Socialist leader, was assassinated on the eve of World War I, after failing to rally the French and German workers to a joint boycott of mobilization in a move to prevent the outbreak of hostilities, revolutionary syndicalism went into eclipse. In subsequent years the rudderless labor movement was gradually politicized by the parties which claimed to speak for industrial labor. Distinct Communist and Catholic national unions evolved following the war to compete with the by-then thoroughly reformist union originally born of revolutionary syndicalism, the *Confédération Générale du Travail* (CGT). The first and the last merged during the period of the Popular Front in the mid-1930s as a measure of solidarity against the threats of domestic fascism, split apart at the start of World War II, reunited during the Resistance, and finally split again in 1947 when the vastly outnumbered reformist workers, including many Socialists, set up their own organization in protest against the authoritarian leadership techniques of the Communists.

Thus, today the French labor movement is politically divided. The strongest union is the now Communist-dominated CGT, with perhaps a million or million and a half members. The CGT is dominant in the primary industries, among the metal workers, and has some following in almost all trades. The *Confédération Française des Travailleurs Chrétiens* (CFTC), closely associated with although not formally related to the MRP, numbers about half a million members. Its greatest importance is regional, in Brittany and the Eastern provinces, but it also boasts significant membership nationally among the railway and textile workers, and in light industry. The smallest national union is the Socialist-oriented *Confédération Générale du Travail—Force Ouvrière* (FO), which draws its chief strength from government and clerical workers. Industrial technicians and foremen are organized separately from the main streams of the labor movement in the *Confédération Générale des Cadres* (CGC). A few occupational groups, such as the teachers, are not only scattered in the principal national unions, but have separate, independent unions of their own.

Compounding the organizational complications and contributing to the disunity of labor is the fact that all three main national unions are normally represented in plants or enterprises of any size, often several competing organizations in a single shop. The great majority of workers are unorganized, although they may lean sympathetically to one central confederation or another. The weakness of the labor movement caused by fragmentation is accentuated by the worker's habit of burdening his union with direct action responsibilities, strikes, protests, demonstrations, etc., to the detriment of the more practical but less stirring bread and butter activities of collective bargaining. This attitude has served to keep French union dues low and thus minimized the range of services the unions can offer their members.

Legislation governing the methods and scope of collective bargaining was among the initial objectives of the Popular Front government of 1936. It was triumphantly obtained in a few hectic days after the French economy had ground to a halt as a result of a wave of nationwide sit-in strikes. The reforms forced through at that time, although somewhat embellished in the immediate post-war period by the Left-dominated Parliament, stand today as the primary base of French industrial relations.

Nearly all bargaining is conducted by trade associations or regional organizations of a single industry on one side of the table and regional or individual subsidiaries of one or more of the national labor unions on the other side. Because it is bitterly opposed by the *Comité National du Patronat Français* (CNPF), the principal French employer association, and because the unions are too weak to insist on it, there is little or no industry-wide bargaining. As a consequence, many different contracts may control wages and working conditions in the same trades in many different regions of France. Government enforcement of collective contracts by Ministry of Labor inspectors can only be invoked if contracts have been "extended," that is, if the terms of a contract hammered out by one set of bargainers are accepted as binding by other employers and their union counterparts who were not involved in the negotiations. However, since extension is not permitted under the law except for a "full contract," i. e., one containing a host of detailed provisions which few unions have the skilled personnel or bargaining power to negotiate, extension is little used.

The government, however, naturally plays an important part in the industrial relations of nationalized industries, and the fact that a large proportion of French workers is on the government's payroll in one form or another has an important effect on the level of private wages. Government enterprises that are monopolies, such as the railways, coal mines, and gas and electric services, are exempt from the workings of the collective bargaining law. In these industries government decrees and regulations govern the conditions of employment and set wage scales. However, in almost all cases the statutes originally adopted to provide a framework for the determination of wages and working conditions contain broad union safeguards, including the right to strike, and allow for considerable negotiation between the union representatives and official management. Government-operated enterprises of a competitive nature, such as insurance companies and aircraft manufacturing plants, are eligible to conduct full collective bargaining. The agreements reached by the bargaining parties must be approved by the boards of directors, on which sit representatives of the government and paradoxically of the unions. Finally, government ministers most directly concerned with government enterprises, of either the competitive or non-competitive sort, may veto wage agreements that they feel will endanger the government's overall economic program. Nevertheless, as an employer the government is considerably more susceptible to pressure for favorable wage adjustments and working conditions than are most private employers, simply because government is normally subject to political demands.

Social Security

In the struggle between revolutionaries and reformists which characterized the early history of French trade unionism, one of the major objectives promised by the reformists was a comprehensive system of social security to provide for the sick, the indigent, or the unemployed worker. No comprehensive plan was ever adopted, but bits and pieces were obtained at different times during the twentieth century until today France boasts a formidable, if not complete, network of social and medical benefits. Some measures were obtained in response to intense labor pressure at given periods, such as the Popular Front or the post-Liberation epoch, when leftist parties controlled Parliament. Other elements of the social security system, particularly the so-called family benefits, were introduced by conservative-oriented governments not with the purpose of supplying a minimum level of dignity for the laborer, but rather to stimulate the French population rate, which had declined to the lowest in Europe between the two world wars. Still other benefits were devised to act as supplements to embarrassingly low industrial and farm wage rates stubbornly maintained by private employers who could not be coerced into undertaking upward revisions by weak governments of the Fourth Republic.

Social security in all its forms is controlled by the Ministry of Labor and the various programs are administered regionally by branch organs, known as *Caisses,* which enjoy financial autonomy, and in some cases actually operate hospitals, clinics, etc., for their members. The *Caisses* are divided into two types, those dealing with social and industrial accident insurance and those charged with administering direct family benefit plans. A national social security agency tops the network of *Caisses*. Social security is supposed to be wholly self-financed in France; insurance charges are shared by both employer and employees; family benefits are financed entirely by levies on employers: the current rate is a sum equivalent to 16.75 per cent of basic wages. Nevertheless, the state must occasionally contribute to the funds of some programs on which—given the curious age distribution of the French population (large numbers of pensioners and infants)—there is a heavy drain.

The most distinctive feature of the French social security system is its decentralized character. Not only are the various elements of the program broken down into individual funds functionally and geographically, but each distinct local unit is supervised and to a certain degree directed by boards whose members are elected, three quarters from the employees benefiting and one quarter from the employers involved. Very often the choice of employee representatives for the available board seats turns into a test of strength between the three major trade union federations, each trying to increase the number of its successful candidates. It is through this mechanism that the Communists, operating through the largest union, the CGT, have maintained an important foothold in semi-official French life.

There would appear to be much in the French social security system for the employer to complain of. He must share or meet all the costs of programs ranging from death and matrimony benefits, hospitalization, and unemployment insurance, and in some enterprises provide paid holidays and transportation allowances. On the other hand, it should be remembered that direct wages are kept low and that benefits under the social security system flow largely to the sick, the older workers, and heads of large families, i. e., to those who pay as much as their younger and unencumbered comrades. As one critic has put it, "The working class functions as a vast mutual aid society in which the poor help out the poorer."

Conclusions

Social welfare in France is obviously a cumbersome and a patchwork business. This is not to say that it cannot work well. Its effectiveness depends in some degree on the vigor of the government in office at any particular moment, but most of all it depends on the longevity of a vigorous government, because its complexity and intricacy require long familiarity before any one set of ministers can master the many levers of control and set the machinery to work in a purposeful way. Failing this the various systems involved are prey to a host of special interests and influences which can exploit weaknesses, loopholes, and long-held privileges to the detriment of the public interest. A study of the distribution and redistribution of income in France as a consequence of the many programs of social welfare, taxation, and direct government intervention in the economy would probably never produce any final or trustworthy statistics. Balancing the total social payments made by one group of the public against the total benefits enjoyed by another group would also be manifestly impossible. Curiously enough, the French with their proclivity for rationalization of all functions, for equipping themselves with the coherent and consistent philosophies that justify their actions and attitudes, have never seen fit to do the same for their public affairs, or at least for the area where their public affairs coincide with their private lives. In fact, the social system and the economy of France resists definition and categorization. They are neither predominantly socialist nor predominantly capitalist. As hybrids they are flexible, adaptable to the changing demands of twentieth century life, but they are without determined direction and careful leadership. They are ill matched against big business, big pressure groups and to a lesser degree big unions—all of which seemingly care little for the national interest.

8 - The Administration, the Judiciary, and Local Government

France is primarily a centralized state. It has been since the days of the *ancien régime*. The corrupt and often ineffective monarchical apparatus of national controls was tidied up and reorganized by Napoleon; the institutions which he and his advisors perfected still survive in the Fifth Republic, only slightly changed. One chronicler of the French administrative machinery tells us that the *Cour des Comptes*—the national organization charged with the review of all official accounting reports and procedures—did not discover the existence of the typewriter and the calculating machine until after World War II. Until the end of the war it used the same quill pens and ledgers that were employed in the *Chambre des Comptes* of the last Capetian kings. The Frenchman's penchant for overburdening the desks of civil servants with the problems of modern society has never changed, nor for that matter has the civil service's spirit of conservatism and traditionalism. As in the past, the national government not only performs the usual functions of administering its own affairs, such as directing foreign relations, operating the public finances, and providing a postal system, but it supervises all local government, and conducts the judicial system. As we have seen in the previous chapter, the state is also deeply involved in the national economy and in nationally sponsored social services.

Although most of the primary government functions are institutionally differentiated, strong personal ties between influential public servants link together the higher branches of government service, and powerful control bodies, still modeled after Napoleonic originals, exercise enormous authority over the entire apparatus and provide a sense of unity. The highest nonpolitical officers of the state have been described as "mandarins who employ their encyclopedic knowledge of the inner workings of the intricate French bureaucratic machinery to insure themselves unlimited, if anonymous power." There is some truth to this. Few private individuals could ever hope to comprehend the complexities of French administration, the various parts of which have taken form at different historical periods in response to particular requirements, each developing distinctive patterns and procedures of its own.

Political leaders, who normally head government ministries, have in general not survived long enough as ministers to acquaint themselves with the mysteries even of their own departments. Very few have had the occasion to probe the great bureaucratic bastions of the judicial system or one of the formidable administrative control bodies, such as the Council of State, whose functions will be considered below. Perhaps the only outsider who might hope to approach a true appreciation of the labyrinthine world of the French state would be a lawyer with long service both as a national deputy and as a local official in his provincial city. Unless, however, his career had been quite an extraordinarily broad one, even he could barely scratch the surface. Curiously enough, the extensive apparatus of the national government, the multitude of civil servants, and even the impressive arbitrary powers which the state exercises, are more or less taken for granted by the highly individualistic Frenchman. He finds it most difficult to understand our federal system with its parallel levels of government, autonomous state administrations, and the overlapping jurisdiction of dissimilar judicial systems. But to say that the French find a unitary apparatus of the state a logically obvious and familiar arrangement tells one very little about their deeper feelings toward the bureaucracy. Indeed the average Frenchman's attitude toward the state, its mysterious authority, and its servants is a curious mixture of resignation, contempt, and envy. For the most part he regards himself as a perpetual loser in a lifelong struggle with authority and its spokesmen. The advantages, he feels, are all on the side of the bureaucrat, but the bureaucrat's actions, in turn, are tightly restricted and controlled by an exacting network of regulations and codes.

The French civil servant is sheltered by the fact that he can only narrowly interpret the regulations which define his functions. He has few opportunities to make errors within the prescribed limits of his job. Moreover, because they are so numerous, the civil servants have over the years developed an impressive array of benefits in pensions, retirement rights, and job security. These aspects of government service are attractive to the average Frenchman, with his deep interest in personal security and *situations acquises*. So, despite general contempt for the arbitrariness and pettiness of the *fonctionnaire* and his position, there is no shortage of applicants for government service. Here then is one of the most curious paradoxes in French political life. By culture, tradition, and political perspective the Frenchman is inclined to suspect the state and its representatives, the civil servants. The smoldering defiance against all forms of authority that is so much a part of the Frenchman's makeup is, of course, primarily aimed against the state in its many guises and expressions. In Algeria today the resentment of working-class settlers against the policies of the de Gaulle government is directed against the symbols of state authority, the Security Police. Perusal of the rosters of the Security Police, however, would reveal a heavy enlistment of Frenchmen, not only from the industrial working class of metropolitan France, but from the proletarian quarters of Algiers. These men personify the ambivalent attitude of the average Frenchman, who both scorns the state and aspires to a job on its payroll.

Administration

The French administrative apparatus is not unified, as in the United States, by the existence of a ubiquitous and homogeneous civil service. Individual departments, although bound in a limited way to observe personnel standards set by the *Direction* of the Public Service (whose enforcement powers are negligible), by and large recruit their own staffs. Advancement to the highest ranks in most departments usually is dependent on possession of a law degree or attendance at the National School of Administration after graduation from a university; there are, however, in many departments provisions for advancement through all grades for the most gifted, regardless of educational background. The highest offices in the bureaucracy are of such stature and importance, nevertheless, that it is a rare individual who can make his way to the post of prefect or permanent secretary-general of a major department without either specialized preparation or the indulgent favors of a political chief. From the permanent staffs of the major departments are chosen the officers of the central control bodies of the state, of which the most important are the Council of State (*Conseil d'Etat*), the Court of Accounts (*Cour de Comptes*), and the Finance Ministry's Inspectorate of Finances. In addition to these bodies a small group of high civil servants, responsible to the Ministry of Interior, serve as prefects, or representatives of the national government, in all of the provinces of France. We shall treat the prefectoral system under the heading Local Government and concern ourselves here only with the important control institutions.

The Council of State, besides having important judicial duties, plays an important role in the legislative and regulation-making function of the government. It reviews laws now in force in France which were passed before the new constitution came into effect to determine whether they fall into the area of legislation or executive regulation. If a law is found to fall in the second category, it can be amended or expanded by simple fiat. The Government must consult with the Council of State in the preparation of executive regulations or decrees, and all Government bills, even of a legislative nature, are laid before the Council. While it is clear that the Council has only an advisory capacity in these matters (the Government can proceed regardless of the Council's opinion), its position and authority are felt throughout the nation. For the vast complex of codes, administrative procedures, and other guidelines of bureaucratic action short of public legislation, the Council of State is the final authority; it issues clear specifications as to how the day-to-day business of government in its relations with the citizenry will be conducted.

Financial accountability within the government is maintained by the Inspectorate of Finances and the Court of Accounts. The former examines all accounts of the various government agencies and to a limited degree therefore supervises their operations and imposes some uniformity of administrative method upon them. The Court of Accounts is primarily charged with a post audit of the government's business, and in the rapidly changing administrations of the Third and Fourth Republics this meant little. Ministers had often departed before a review of ministry conduct could be made public. It remains to be seen whether under the more stable conditions of the Fifth Republic the court's reports will have greater significance. Finally, it should be noted that from the corps of elite civil servants occupying positions in the control bodies of the state, political leaders can and do choose men to carry out important or unusual assignments, or to fill positions in their personal staffs. President de

Gaulle has carried this practice to its logical conclusion by bestowing cabinet rank on several prominent civil servants, most notably Maurice Couve de Murville as Foreign Minister and Louis Joxe as Minister for Algeria. This practice, while it may tend to politicize the officers involved, can also be regarded as an efficient use of some of France's most brilliant talent.

As noted, the national government performs a myriad of functions affecting the daily life of every Frenchman, provides him with many services, and controls his conduct in numerous ways. The Frenchman is confronted by representatives of the national government far more frequently than he is by local officers, whose powers and responsibilities are severely limited. Until quite recently each national department or ministry set up its local or branch offices wherever the need for it existed, ranging from the almost universal *bureaus* of the postal, telephone, and telegraph services to the widely scattered *Offices des Régions Météorologiques.* All too often, however, significant decisions had to be referred back to Paris; there was little opportunity for the development of personal initiative, or for that matter the development of careers outside of the capital city. The Fifth Republic has taken a timid step forward in the effort to solve both the problems of overlapping and inconsistent jurisdictions and the stagnation of the field services. Overlaying the ninety-two departments into which the political map of France has long been divided there are now twenty-one primary administrative districts. These conform generally to the traditional regional areas such as Brittany, Normandy, Burgundy, etc., historically associated with distinct geographic or political entities. None of the new districts cut across departmental boundaries, but instead each district encompasses several full departments. It is anticipated that most of the principal operations of the national government will be grouped within these districts, although clearly there must be considerable flexibility in the new arrangements. Thus the *Bureau de Conservation des Eaux et Forêts* will be allowed to further subdivide the districts into some forty subdivisions, and the aforementioned Meteorological Service will group several districts into larger ones, giving it a total of only four districts. The important fields of education, customs, taxation, justice, and public order are so far exempt from this regrouping and reorganization of field services.[1] As yet no district capitals have been designated,

[1] The French educational system is uniquely decentralized. There are eighteen geographic units, each under the general supervision of one of the great national universities located within its confines.

nor is any national officer or commission authorized to supervise the districts. Nevertheless, this first move in rationalizing the clumsy French administrative services in the field may foreshadow further progress toward decentralization when the government feels that vested interests within the bureaucracy can be persuaded of its value.

The Judiciary

The French judicial system differs widely from our own; the justice it dispenses is derived from minutely recorded codes, not from a blend of accumulated customs, precedents, and reason as in Anglo-Saxon jurisprudence. Judges and prosecutors alike are servants of the state, but the President of the Republic is constitutionally charged with guaranteeing the independence of the judicial authority and occupies the presidency of the Superior Council of Justice. Indeed, the whole judicial apparatus and its proceedings are wrapped in a jealously guarded dignity designed to protect them from charges of political influence. French history contains a dreary record of magistrates being used to support the political requirements of revolutionary leaders, or, on the opposite extreme, as instruments for the protection of a propertied and monied class against the legal assaults of a republic considered dangerously egalitarian. Hence the conscious effort in recent years to provide the judiciary with an atmosphere of detachment, an effort that has been largely successful, although it has at times tended to bureaucratize the judiciary and to make it more dependent on expertise than on wisdom.

A distinctive quality of the French judicial system is its division into two primary fields: the normal jurisdiction concerned with the citizen's relations to his fellows, criminal acts, and civil cases; the other a special administrative jurisdiction concerned exclusively with the acts of government officials or state employees accused of overstepping their authority or otherwise damaging the rights of private citizens. There are separate hierarchies of courts for each of the two jurisdictions and a Tribunal of Conflicts composed of high judges from both hierarchies to determine in which system a case rightfully belongs in the event a dispute arises. This dual quality of French jurisprudence dates back to 1789 and provides the strongest defense of the Frenchman's individual rights against an immensely powerful and ubiquitous state. As we have observed earlier, the civil rights of French citizens are nowhere as clearly stated as they are in the United

States Bill of Rights and subsequent amendments. The constitution of the Fifth Republic reiterates the republic's attachment to both the "Rights of Man" as defined in 1789 and the somewhat fuller specifications contained in the preamble to the constitution of 1946, but beyond these rather generalized guarantees, there are no constitutional provisions which detail precisely how human liberties are to be preserved. Accordingly, the existence of an elaborate, separate, and distinctive body of law limiting the activities of state officials is a fundamental safeguard against the development of arbitrary executive power.

THE CIVIL AND CRIMINAL COURTS. Civil and criminal cases are tried by a common body of officers, known collectively as the Magistracy, in which there are clearly defined ranks and schedules of promotions, and to which entry is normally restricted to young men with law degrees just beginning their life's work. The Magistracy is in every sense a career service. In addition to the judges the service includes state officers known as *parquets,* who act as prosecutors, but whose functions are so closely related to those of the judges themselves that they are known as members of the standing judiciary (*la magistrature debout*). From time to time and as they proceed upward in rank, careerists may serve as minor judges, substitute *parquets,* officials in the Ministry of Justice, or be assigned back to the bench at a higher level or to a more important prosecutor's office. Members of the administrative courts are, however, recruited separately, by the *Conseil d'Etat,* the highest administrative tribunal.

Civil cases are heard in the 454 Courts of First Instance (*Tribunal d'Instance*) or, if the case involves substantial sums, in one of the Courts of Great Instance (*Tribunal de Grande Instance*). The latter court also has some appeal functions, especially from the judgments of special technical courts set up to determine workers' rights under individual labor contracts and commercial tribunals operated and maintained by associations of business people to resolve disputes between businessmen. Courts of the First Instance are presided over by a single judge who, in addition to his more formal powers, also functions much as a justice of the peace did in the past, settling domestic and other minor disputes by conciliation, or occasionally by fiat. Each court is staffed with a *parquet* and one or more assistants who work closely with the magistrate in the preparation and dispatch of judicial business. Courts of Great Instance have three or more judges sitting *en banc,* but neither they nor the lower civil courts employ juries.

Criminal law is dispensed in one of three sets of courts, depending on the gravity of the offense. Police courts function in almost all localities of any importance for minor infractions. More serious offenses are brought before Correctional Courts where, without benefit of a jury, judges can impose punishments ranging up to five years' imprisonment. Finally, major felonies and crimes are tried at periodic sittings of the *Cours d'Assises* (Assize Courts), which consist of three judges and nine special jurors. Eight votes of the twelve are required for conviction, and French judges normally bring their influence strongly to bear on the jurors. In fact the French judge is by no means an impartial figure; he actively participates in the questioning of defendants and witnesses, instructs the *parquet* on tactics, and feels no compulsion to conceal his own opinions in a given case. Nevertheless, the procedure is fair in its own right, and generally the magistrates are highly skilled in the intricacies of courtroom procedure. As the career system operates, the justices cannot afford to have their records spotted with too many decisions struck down by higher courts for failing to observe proper procedures.

Actually French law allows only one appeal in civil and criminal cases. For the former, appeal can be made from either Courts of First Instance or Great Instance to one of several Appeal Courts, which are divided into panels according to the subject of the litigation in question. Criminal cases from lower courts may be appealed to the Assize Court but no further; hence there is no effective appeal possible for a case initiated at the Assize Court. However, a peculiar exception to the one appeal rule exists. If a pure matter of law is in dispute, i. e., the interpretation of a lower court judge as to what the law in a given case is, the matter can be brought to France's highest judicial body, the Court of Cassation. This unique institution simply decides the point of law in question and directs that the case be retried in a lower court if either party so wishes it. The Court of Cassation never hears or judges a complete case itself.

Overseeing this formidable judicial structure—and theoretically assisting the President of the Republic in his duties as guarantor of the independence of the judiciary—is the Superior Council of the Judiciary. A similar institution existed under the Fourth Republic. It had been designed to serve as a buffer between the individual officers serving the system and their nominal superior, the minister of justice, in the hope that it would eliminate the chance of courts being politicized by the too rapid advancement of judges eager to do a minister's bidding. On the whole the candidates selected for the original Council were sound, professional jurists and leading lawyers, but as a body the Council lacked the political strength to assert its authority. Under the present constitutional arrangements the President of the Republic selects all the members (save the minister of justice, who is *ex-officio* vice-president of the Council). He chooses six members from nominations presented to him by the judicial profession, one member from the *Conseil d'Etat* and nominated by it, and two other members who have no connections with the judiciary. The Council, besides its role as adviser to the president, also nominates appointees for the Court of Cassation, reviews other promotions in the system proposed by the minister of justice, and counsels the president on his exercise of the pardon. It is too soon to evaluate this institution in its new dress, but it certainly appears to have drawn strength from close identity with the president. Nevertheless, while parliamentary influence at least has been completely eliminated, presidential influence could easily become overwhelming.

Finally, a word should be said about the existence in France (at this writing still under emergency conditions imposed by the continuation of the Algerian war) of military tribunals which operate quite independently of the normal judicial system and are frequently concerned with cases involving fundamental human rights and individual liberties. The rules of procedure employed in these courts are patterned after those in the traditional criminal courts, but there all similarity ends. The judges are for the most part military officers; such vital questions as the period of detention for suspects, indictment procedures, and the responsibility of witnesses are decided on the basis of military expediency, which in most cases in a country engaged in an unpopular war can be translated to mean political expediency. Critics in France have already charged that these courts are distorting the true quality of justice and that, since the public fails to distinguish between military and civilian courts, the use of the former as political instruments threatens sooner or later to destroy the prestige and independence of the latter.[2]

THE ADMINISTRATIVE COURTS. The separate institutions provided for the adjudication of administrative faults are far simpler than those of the traditional judiciary, but the legal questions

[2] Acting under Article 16 of the constitution, President de Gaulle authorized in April 1961 the establishment of a special high military court with extraordinary powers and few limits on its authority to try mutineers of the abortive military revolt in Algeria.

involved are often highly complex. By and large, administrative jurisprudence revolves around questions concerning what the French call *excés du pouvoir.* This refers to the problem of an official's overstepping the limits of his responsibilities and injuring private interests in some way. Similarly, any failure to act by a civil servant which results in damages can be used as the basis for charges against the official. The determination of whether a public official is personally responsible for the improper acts he has committed, or whether the public service for which he was acting failed to properly guide, instruct, or limit him, are examples of the questions on which administrative courts may have to rule. If an official is found personally responsible, he can be prosecuted or sued in the criminal or civil courts; if the system is at fault the state pays an indemnity to the citizen wronged by the action of its official. The law on which such judgments are rendered is compiled in massive texts of administrative jurisprudence by the elite body of high bureaucrats, the *Conseil d'Etat* (Council of State).

The Council is, as the Superior Council of the Judiciary, headed by the President of the Republic, and its vice-chairman is the minister of justice. However, in this case the president actually participates only on rare ceremonial occasions and the main work and leadership of the Council is undertaken by its 149 professional members. These men are chosen from among the highest officials of the principal ministries and from the prefectural corps. In addition, a few younger men, who are legal specialists from the Ministry of Justice, are members of the Council. The membership of the Council fluctuates as various officials, having served a term on its deliberative panels, return to active administrative posts in the service from which they originally came. Once having served on the Council, however, they are usually marked for an illustrious climax to their careers, either as the permanent undersecretaries of government ministries, or as super-prefects, charged with the supervision of several departments, or possibly in some specialized function, such as Delegate General for Algeria, an office which in effect represents the authority of the President of the Republic.

The work of the Council is by no means confined to adjudication. As we have already seen, it has responsibilities *vis à vis* Parliament and must deliver frequent opinions on the content of planned legislation. It participates in the drafting of all government decrees and orders. Furthermore the Council acts as a watchdog of the whole national administrative machinery in

France and resolves jurisdictional tangles which may arise between two or more ministries. Only the *Section des Contentieux* (Section of Disputes) of the Council actually operates as a court to review cases in administrative law. Most important cases come directly to one of several panels of administrative magistrates into which the Section of Disputes is divided. However, the case load since World War II has been so heavy that lesser courts were set up in 1953 in several prefectural districts under the general supervision of the Council to eliminate the more routine problems. The Council itself, however, acts as a general court of appeal for judgments rendered at the prefectural level.

The operation of the system contains an obvious paradox. On the one hand the French citizen is provided with fairly direct legal recourse against the actions of government officials who may have overstepped their authority in dealing with him—a process, incidentally, both easier and cheaper than the system for bringing suit against the government available to United States citizens. On the other hand, the determination as to whether his complaint is worthy of a hearing, the standards by which the offensive act is adjudged, and the final decision in the case, are all in the hands of the highest members of that same officialdom which includes in its ranks the civil servant or servants who originally committed the offense. Not only are those who sit in judgment officials themselves, but they may have an intimate connection with the ministry where the incident under scrutiny originated. Despite this curious legal situation, however, standards of fairness on the administrative tribunals are high—one suspects that the time-honored prestige of the *Conseil d'État* is sufficient to dispel charges of bureaucratic arbitrariness or obscurantism.

Local Government

France is a heterogeneous land, geographically, economically, and culturally as diverse as several distinct countries. Some corners of the nation are sparsely populated and sunk in a marginal and still crude subsistence agriculture; elsewhere there are highly industrialized or commercialized urban centers surrounded by both tenement districts and suburbia. In addition, of course, there are the great cosmopolitan European cities of Paris, Lyons, Rouen, and Strasbourg and the busy ports of Marseilles, Bordeaux, Nantes, and Brest. Despite this diversity France has never developed effective local governments that would give expression to particular interests and peculiar regional problems and needs.

Tutelage from Paris is the principal theme of the system of local government. Where control from the capital is not directly asserted by prefects responsible to the Ministry of Interior, it is effected by the use of grants-in-aid from the national ministries to impoverished localities. The authority of Paris is rarely absent even down to the minutest detail of local administration and services.

The basic political unit of the local community—whether it be a remote village of a few score souls or a large city such as Toulouse—is the commune. Only twenty-four of the nearly 40,000 communes in France have over 100,000 inhabitants, while well over 3,000 have 100 or less. Each commune is governed by an elected municipal council whose size depends on the population it serves. However, even the smallest commune is entitled to eleven councillors while communes of over 60,000 inhabitants have only thirty-seven. Each council elects a mayor from its membership who becomes the executive officer of the community and is charged with carrying out those government functions reserved for the communes: public education, social welfare, police, fire protection, and housekeeping duties for official buildings and properties. National law requires that each community maintain these basic services, and it should be noted that the locality has little freedom in controlling the services it is obliged to provide. The Ministry of Education, for example, keeps a careful check on the quality of education offered; the welfare services are primarily national programs administered in only a few details by local authorities. Central control over the mayor and the council is exercised by the prefect in most matters, and in the smaller communes by subprefects. The prefect must approve the municipal budget prepared by the mayor, but if a serious conflict develops it is the *Conseil d'Etat* in Paris which decides whether a municipality may or may not undertake some action, or has or has not performed its obligatory responsibilities correctly. Moreover the financial accounts of all communes are subject to review by the *Cour des Comptes,* a process which imposes a national system of bookkeeping and financing on every municipal council.

The next level of local administration, and a more important political unit than that of the municipal council, is the General Council of each of the ninety-two departments. An aspiring political figure often uses a seat on his departmental General Council as a springboard for obtaining a National Assembly or Senate seat. Political parties are organized locally at the departmental level; hence, although there are few practical administrative responsibilities for the General Council to perform, it is nevertheless an active and sometimes turbulent center of French political life. The size of the individual council depends on the number of cantons into which the particular department is divided. Since the departments of France were artificially divided into cantons many decades ago when the population was spread thinly about the surface of the country, and because there has been little serious redistricting since, the recently developed and thickly populated urban areas are grossly under-represented on most General Councils.

The departmental councils provide a delicately engineered but necessary link between the national government and the primary structure of French society. Although the geographical divisions represented by the departments do not necessarily conform to either traditional regions, such as Normandy or Provençe, nor to existing natural economic and social contours, they have nevertheless over the years developed a quality and spirit of their own. Thus a resident of the department of Calvados who has determined opinions about the peculiar needs of his department may expect some recognition of these needs in his departmental council, and his requirements may differ sharply from those of the lifelong inhabitant of the Landes department. The departmental council is charged with the local administration of many nationally sponsored services and with the development of departmental services, such as the local highway network. In these matters it can adjust its operations to the distinctive tastes and needs of its own area, although always of course, within fairly narrow limits set in Paris. The council also assists the communes of the department with the provision of basic services and aids them in undertaking cooperative ventures through the allocation of departmental funds.

The prefect plays a unique and leading part in the political life of his department, although he is not an elected official. He serves as executive officer of the General Council, but is not its president, who is elected from the council's membership. On the other hand the prefect attends all meetings, prepares the departmental budget and may, if he chooses, by suggesting policies, play an aggressive role in stimulating the council's departmental activities. Or he can, if the council is in the hands of an effective political leader, or one with whom he basically disagrees, but who is correctly fulfilling his obligatory responsibilities, assume a largely passive role. Many of the more important decisions concerning the department's business, especially those involving the expenditure of large amounts of public funds, are made in any event in the offices of the Ministry of the Interior. In such decisions a skillful and trusted prefect with a strong record of past accomplishment in other departments can usually make his voice and his opinions felt in Paris. On the other hand the councillors may be important politicians in their own right (not infrequently serving also as national deputies) and may be in a position to exert direct political pressures on Paris ministries in behalf of interests affecting their home departments. On balance, of course, the effective prefect attempts to conduct his relations with the General Council of his department in such a way that power struggles do not develop and so that he personally comes to symbolize a cooperative, albeit a powerful partner in resolving the problems and meeting the demands of the local area.

Finally, a word should be said about police organization in France and the special police powers of the prefectural corps. Municipalities are responsible for providing their own police protection. Police commissioners operate under the authority of the mayor, but are appointed by the prefect, who thereby maintains at least an indirect control over all police functions in his district. According to the importance of his department (i. e., if important cities are located within it), the prefect has specific authority to direct the activities of the local police. In addition three bodies of national police are found in France: (1) The *Sûreté Nationale* operates under the guidance of the Ministry of Interior and is responsible for internal security throughout the country. Plainclothes officers of the Sûreté may be called in by prefects or local authorities in case of need. (2) The *Gendarmerie* are organized on semi-military lines into strongly armed companies of national security, which are posted in various parts of France. They are available for use in any locality on the call of the prefect and have been employed often to contain strikes, guard against sabotage, and to restrain political demonstrations. Several of these companies are now in Algeria, serving in the so-called "pacified areas" to guard against the return of rebel influence and also to handle settler and Moslem demonstrations against the policy of the metropolitan government. (3) Under the general supervision of the Paris prefect of police[3] a national police force serves Paris, its suburbs, and several of the other

[3] The city of Paris has two prefects: one the regular civil administrator, the other a powerful figure who serves as a sort of super police commissioner and is responsible for the security of the city and hence of the national government.

large cities. This force is controlled by the Ministry of the Interior and is partly financed by the cities it serves and partly by the ministry. For emergencies a special force called the *Garde Républicaine,* which is also used for ceremonial occasions and for protecting the president's palace and other key buildings, is available. In addition to putting these multiple police services at the disposal of its prefects, the central government has organized the entire country into a few super-prefectural districts, each embracing several departments. These districts are headed by senior prefects, who in the event of a national emergency become virtual proconsuls for the whole of their districts. All police, both local and national, and all the armed forces billeted in the district of a super-prefect come immediately under his command, an arrangement which has not yet been fully tested in any situation where the police and the military might be expected to differ on the orders they were required to implement. The existence of this system, its effectiveness, and the loyalty of the super-prefects to the authority of Paris, could become crucial if France became involved in civil war, or the threat of civil war, over some deeply divisive issue, such as the government's policies for ending the Algerian war.

9 - Foreign Policy

French foreign policy derives its force, direction, and style from Charles de Gaulle. However, having made this generalization, we cannot conclude that it is uniquely his creation, for the general, better than any other figure in modern France, understands the strength and usefulness of the past. If there is a key to comprehending France's present foreign policy, it is to be found in de Gaulle's appreciation of his country's history. He has readily admitted that at times in the twentieth century France came to the bargaining table of international politics with no material or military substance, no assets in the accepted currency of international relations, and yet she maintained her position and indeed often strengthened it. This does not mean that France dealt alone in the faded glories of past greatness—a manifest impossibility in the cold world of international diplomacy. What it does mean is that France has demonstrated through de Gaulle that diplomatic technique, firm leadership, world influence (if not world power), although overlooked in recent decades, if skillfully employed can be indices of international status only slightly less formidable than vast populations, great national wealth, giant industrial complexes, and large standing military establishments. What de Gaulle has done is to emphasize the best of France's assets, all of which have their roots in the past: her world-wide cultural influence, the traditional intelligence of her people, the energy of her leaders, and a crucial geographic position on the crossroads of Western Europe. From this amalgam he has created the image of a vibrant, living State with a special character and force that he is busily adapting to the requirements of an otherwise bi-polar world.

There is no trickery in all this because France is accepted as a power on the international stage to an extent which nations of roughly comparable size and equivalent richness in historical tradition, such as Spain and even Japan, are not. One reason for this, of course, is that de Gaulle has insisted on asserting his claim for French *grandeur*. Furthermore, he has never desisted from forcing his claim on the other nations of the world which are sufficiently endowed with the natural and tangible elements of power to make their recognition of his claim decisive. Spain and Japan, on the other hand, have generally preferred the seclusion forced on them since the days of World War II; as their pretensions have been limited, so have their international positions been confined to secondary and even tertiary roles. While de Gaulle has not used sleight of hand in carving out a unique status for France, he has not hesitated to capitalize on the mystique of his own person to achieve the goals he has set for his country.

Although essential to the task of restoring the glory of France, the fact that de Gaulle's part in the effort is dominant constitutes its greatest fragility. Before analyzing the international drives of French foreign policy, one perhaps preliminary observation must be made at this point: the discussion of French foreign policy which follows depends on the survival either of General de Gaulle personally, or on the successful implantation of the image of France he is fostering. If he should pass from the scene suddenly, before the nature of his effort was fully appreciated and accepted by the great majority of the French people, it is quite possible that the international assets to which he has given new meaning and value would be quickly swept away.

Postwar French Foreign Policy

To understand the position of France in the modern world and the status which de Gaulle claims for his country, it is necessary to return to the days coincident with the end of World War II in Europe. France, although technically counted among the allied victors against the Third German Reich, was in fact only a shell. She had been humiliated by the sudden defeat imposed by the *Wehrmacht* in 1940. In the process of fighting the German invader and in subsequent years of allied bombings much of the nation's wealth had been destroyed. The restoration of French sovereignty, moreover, had been largely accomplished by the force of American and British arms, and indirectly, by the Russian armies, which broke Hitler's Eastern front. France played only a secondary role in these events, despite General de Gaulle's success in fielding a Liberation army of surprising size, largely composed of Frenchmen from the overseas empire in Africa, the Middle East, and Indo-China.

Once the fighting ceased in Europe, France saw her holdings elsewhere threatened not by the erstwhile enemy, but by her allies and by the newly born forces of native nationalism. Under British pressure she was quickly forced to dissolve her protectorates in the Levant, and shortly thereafter began despatching troops to Indo-China to quell incipient native revolt in Viet Nam. By the late 1940s nationalist stirrings began in North Africa. Within a few years Tunisia and Morocco had won their independence, and the disastrous Indo-Chinese war was succeeded by an even more agonizing struggle in Algeria which continues at this writing.

Meanwhile, in Europe proper France was involved in a somewhat footless search for security against the possible revival of German militarism, to which she had fallen victim three times in less than a century. At the same time she was seeking a means of maintaining the leadership of the continent, when ill-prepared to do so. Preoccupation with the German question made it difficult for French policy makers to grasp the essential fact that in a world where an uneasy balance of power was delicately kept between the United States and the Soviet Union, neither of these two great nations would allow Germany to become a pawn of the other. Hence the only solution from the point of view of *real-politik* was to see to it that the West's particular half of Germany did not become dangerously weak relative to the other half and, more importantly, to positively commit the weight of the Bonn Republic to the power of the West. The long detour of French foreign policy before this fact was realized complicated and delayed the effective building of a united Europe, and caused antagonism against France throughout Europe and the Free World.

Nevertheless, considerable progress was made in the early years after the war toward bringing Europe closer together, and France instigated most of these moves. She was instrumental in initiating international discussions which led to the creation of the Council of Europe, the European Coal and Steel Community, and contributed effectively to the international planning which produced the Organization for European Economic Cooperation (OEEC). Although France moved with dispatch and provided ingenious leadership during the formative periods of these organizations, the path was by no means smooth, and considerable European suspicion of French motives resulted. These suspicions were roused because the French saw a unified Europe first as a means of controlling a renascent Germany and secondly as a third force between the Soviets and the United States. The British, closely linked to the United States by tradition and after World War II by shared responsibility for nuclear development, were naturally irked by the evident objectives of Paris. Preoccupied with Commonwealth relations and the elaboration of her ambitious domestic welfare program, Great Britain consistently hampered French initiatives. However, it was finally American insistence on employing German power to balance Soviet pressure from the East which changed the direction of French foreign policy. When the French realized that the United States considered Germany rehabilitated, a fundamental *raison d'être* of French foreign policy was suddenly snuffed out. From that time forward the twin goals of containing Germany and of creating a European third force began to lose their substance. Moreover, there were no new goals to take their place—at least until the return of de Gaulle to power—and a great deal of frantic patching up suddenly needed doing throughout the collapsing empire. Thus, from the period of about 1950 to 1958 French foreign policy had no clear focus save that of conserving a dwindling position, both in the overseas territories, and in world opinion.

EDC—A Turning Point

The most dramatic illustration of the French confusion over foreign policy objectives which characterized the last years of the Fourth Republic was the National Assembly's rejection of the European Defense Community Treaty (EDC) in 1954. This episode, coming hard on the heels of French defeat in Indo-China, constituted the low point of France's long and frustrating postwar search for a leading role in world affairs. Great Britain had early indicated she would refuse to join the French-inspired concept of a common European military establishment; the United States had decided on German rearmament despite French misgivings and protests. Moreover, France was also faced with Germany's rising challenge while her energies were consumed in distant battlefields and at least half her armed forces deployed overseas. France had overextended herself and, facing a modest future, found herself deeply troubled over what that future should be. The immediate consequence of the defeat of EDC was to hasten the search by the United States and Great Britain for means of incorporating Germany into NATO on a national basis. Within a matter of weeks after the Assembly's action the long moribund Brussels Pact for European defense had been revived; Italy and Germany had been added to its membership, and the whole complex welcomed into NATO in a neat diplomatic maneuver engineered by the British Foreign Secretary, Anthony Eden.

The EDC treaty represented the final effort of French statesmen to minimize the impact of German rearmament—on which the United States was insisting as a means of strengthening NATO—by integrating continental European armed forces into one military establishment which would operate under a supranational political authority controlled by the governments of the participants. In this way the treaty's original sponsors hoped that the inevitable course of Germany's revival as a military power would be channeled to facilitate European defense rather than German aggression. The debate within France, which was conducted on several levels, both national and international, and by a variety of French governments, ranged over a period of four years. In the end the treaty was defeated in the National Assembly by a coalition of indignant nationalists under the whip of the Gaullist Debré, Socialists, Communists, and a scattering of deputies from the Center and Right who either felt the treaty would be meaningless without British participation or who hoped that by voting "no" they could somehow delay the rearming of Germany.

From this point until the coming of de Gaulle, French foreign policy tended to take a back seat to domestic and colonial affairs. However, while the politicians were preoccupied by events in Algeria, which eventually brought on the death of the Fourth Republic, the French foreign office was free to pursue the limited goal of European unity through the functional approach. In the mid-fifties treaties for the pan-European development of atomic energy and for a common economic market were prepared and negotiated by professional French technicians and diplomats and ratified by a singularly disinterested National Assembly. These were, however, measures which would not be implemented until 1959 when a new regime was in power in Paris and when the focus of French foreign policy had been radically altered. Nevertheless, the fact that French officials, despite the rebuff of the Assembly in rejecting the Defense Community Treaty, pressed on with their long-range plans to draw Europe closer together, indicated that the notion of French leadership in Europe was by no means dead. It also meant that when the new government of General de Gaulle took power it was presented with a *fait accompli*—a clearly marked signpost bearing the legend "European Unity," which the de Gaulle regime accepted as a legacy it could not afford to shrug off at once.

France and European Integration

This powerful impulse toward integration in Europe has in fact been one of the most awkward traditions with which de Gaulle has had to cope since his assumption of power. Integration is in many ways contrary to de Gaulle's basic philosophy on the nature of foreign policy. Quite simply, he holds the view that all foreign relations are a function of the interaction of national interests. All states must be assumed to operate on the basis of what promotes their national interest; any failure along this line compromises the international position which a state desires to fill, any failure to appreciate the national interest of another state risks precipitating a fundamental error in foreign policy.

Using these harsh guidelines, de Gaulle had asserted France's claim to great-power status during the darkest hours of French history in World War II. He had succeeded in having his armies recognized as independent military forces not subject to control by allied field commanders; he had secured recognition of his government as the legitimate vehicle for French sovereignty, and he had assured the admission of France as an occupying power in defeated Germany and as a veto power on the Security Council of the United Nations. Quite naturally, he felt that his nationalistic views of power and its prerogatives had proved their worth, and that the new mid-century emphasis on integration of European economic and political institutions as an end in itself was highly questionable. Consequently, de Gaulle found the strength of French sentiment for European unification both surprising and distasteful. He was, however, finally persuaded that not only was the context of European politics changing slowly, but that there were distinct advantages for France written into some of the integration treaties. Hence he somewhat reluctantly lent his prestige, at least temporarily, to the support and defense of integration. The movement toward integration was the great French contribution to Europe in the years since World War II, but it has been largely overshadowed by subsequent pressure toward a stronger emphasis on nationalism which, as we will see below, while it does not threaten France's participation in the institutions of which she is a member, probably precludes French extension of integration into other fields.

The most far-reaching undertaking in the direction of European unity that France has taken is her agreement to participate in the European Economic Community, or the Common Market, as it is more popularly called. The participants, which include besides France, Germany, Italy, Belgium, Holland, and Luxembourg, have agreed to throw open their domestic markets to the trade and commerce of all the members, and have committed themselves to specific timetables for the reduction of tariffs, quotas, and internal subsidies that have operated in the past as controls on the interchange of economic traffic between them. Moreover, the treaty setting up the Common Market obliges each of the members to accept a single set of controls for all trade outside of the Community. Further equalization of competitive conditions between members is contemplated in the treaty by the explicit obligation undertaken by the signers to work out means of obtaining a free movement of labor from one state to another and equalizing social security systems in all six.

By adhering to the Common Market France swept away a long tradition of centering its international economic policies on domestic protectionism. Significantly, the step was taken when, as we have noted above, the primary French objectives of limiting German revival and of assuming undisputed leadership of continental Europe had met with sharp if not definitive reversals. In other words economic integration was pursued not only for its own sake, but probably more importantly, out of a sense of Gallic realism: if the revival of Germany could not be halted, then German prosperity should be put to use in such a way as to aid the French economy. The French business community, although by no means of one voice on the matter, did not oppose the measure as strongly as it might have during the period immediately after the war, when the industrial plant was all but inoperative and the specter of German competition constantly haunted the more leisurely French producer and trader. By the late nineteen fifties a psychological change had made itself felt in France—and many individual businessmen welcomed French membership in the EEC as a means of gaining access to a far greater market for the sale of their goods.

Germany, however, was made to pay the price for French cooperation by being forced to agree to a number of special advantages for France. Agriculture was specifically exempted from the terms of the treaty. Moreover, a large development fund for the expansion of economic enterprise in the overseas territories of the members was set up. Germany, with no foreign holdings of her own, agreed to contribute a goodly share of the fund, the great bulk of which was earmarked for the development of French African territories. Thus, whereas the movement for integration of Europe in the early postwar years had been largely at the insistence of France, this important step of the late nineteen fifties would not have been possible without German statesmanship. The tortuously slow advances in this field have changed the nature of Franco-German relationships and have made the entente between Paris and Bonn the central arch of European stability. In addition, the strong ties between France and West Germany, developed since the collapse of the Defense Community project in 1954, have undoubtedly had impressive political consequences, despite the frustration of other French foreign policy objectives concerning Germany. Many Frenchmen now believe that as long as the links between the two countries remain effective—and mutually advantageous—there is less chance that West Germany will be tempted to abandon Europe, join its Eastern counterpart, and adopt a policy of nationalist *revanchism.*

France and NATO

For the French, membership in NATO has been regarded as both an international necessity and a meaningful protection against any Soviet threat to take over the continent. On the one hand, France is most anxious to keep United States forces in Europe and retain the specific American commitment to come to the defense of any NATO member endangered by Soviet attack. On the other hand France, resenting the special mutual defense arrangements joining the United States and Great Britain, has sought to emphasize the international character of her national responsibilities and receive special recognition for them in the alliance. She has demanded that the NATO Council extend its discussions of Western strategy to include Africa and the Near East as well as the Soviet bloc. She hoped, when embarking on the abortive invasion of Suez in 1956 in collaboration with the British, that the United States and other members of the alliance would tacitly accept France's national prerogative to punish Egypt for its aid to the Algerian rebellion. Most determinedly of all, however, France has insisted on NATO recognition of her special position in Africa. Germany has been willing to go along with this claim, but the United States, hesitant to affront the newly emergent independent African states, has consistently refused to satisfy French demands. Paradoxically, however, France has refrained from submitting the Algerian problem to NATO jurisdiction; she is neither willing to risk allied criticism of some of her policies in the area, nor prepared to admit that as a great power France cannot manage her own domestic affairs.

Thus, France finds herself in an awkward position in NATO, a position which is a function of the conflict between the role she casts for herself and her opportunities to fulfill that role. France has never met her NATO quota of fourteen army divisions for continental defense because the bulk of her armed forces was either in Indo-China or in Algeria; moreover, she has seen a German general put in command of European ground forces in recognition of the increasing strength of the German contribution to the alliance. She has been rebuffed in her efforts to expand the responsibilities of the alliance to cover situations where she insisted—as in Suez, Indo-China, and Africa—she was doing as much to strengthen the West against communism as any member short of the United States. In essence then, the

French attitude toward NATO is mixed. While she regards alliance with the United States as an essential for security she also feels it inhibits the accomplishment of other objectives of French foreign policy, and frustrates the assertion of France's standing as an independent international force.

De Gaulle's Effect on French Foreign Policy

It is appropriate to introduce consideration of de Gaulle's impact on French foreign policy at this point because it is so often associated simply with France's increasingly stiff-necked attitude within the NATO alliance. Certainly the general has rewritten the code of behavior for the Foreign Ministry, or *Quai d'Orsay,* as it is called. But de Gaulle has done much more than this. He has given not only a new tone to the conduct of French foreign relations, but has capitalized on the efforts of the premiers and foreign ministers who filled the years between his first exercise of public office during the war years and his second beginning in 1958. To the somewhat ill-defined aspirations and gropings of these interim administrations he has imposed a purpose and direction, largely through the use of his own powerful personality and diplomatic skill. In short he has suggested to his countrymen and to the world that France has an historic role to fill on the international scene and that it is being played continuously, not without setbacks and disappointments, sometimes more effectively than at other times, but always according to a pattern or order which is defined by the existence of the nation state of France herself. By this he means the position of France, her history, her national assets, and her world-wide influence. In the final lines of the memoirs of his World War II experiences de Gaulle reflectively summarized his views on the continuing nature of France's greatness: "Old France, overwhelmed by history, body bruised by wars and by revolutions, vacillating endlessly from grandeur to decline, but set to rights again from one century to the next by the spirit of renewal." [1]

This, then, is the perspective from which present-day French foreign policy is conducted—historical, patient, and intensely confident. The tone is heavily nationalistic, but realistic also in the sense that periods of weakness and recuperation are recognized as necessary interludes interspersed between the

[1] Memoirs—*Le Salut,* T. III, p. 290.

normal situation of French grandeur. We have said that de Gaulle employed all the elements of his predecessors in designing France's foreign policy. On careful examination there is nothing new in the objectives he has set for France; he has, however, evoked a much wider sense of public optimism and confidence in the achievement of these goals. The objectives themselves are clear: recognition of great power status and a concomitant broad degree of national independence, which in the immediate context of world affairs means less reliance on the United States; leadership in continental Europe of a bloc of countries that reduces the direct abrasive contact between the Soviet world and what de Gaulle calls the Anglo-Saxon powers; a dominant influence in Africa as the tutor and companion of new states nourished on French culture and French political ideals. The general has advanced on all three fronts, although at this writing it is still difficult to measure the degree of his success or its permanence.

De Gaulle's first moves in establishing France as a great power were, as we have already seen, taken during the war years. He has, however, resumed the same path fifteen years later by loosening what he regarded as the limiting shackles of the NATO treaty. France has not repudiated the treaty nor renounced her obligations under it, but has instead led a campaign to change the nature of the alliance. In the Gaullist conception NATO should become the strategic headquarters for all Western policies aimed at blocking Communist expansion throughout the world. The three states with world-wide responsibilities, the United States, Great Britain, and France, should accordingly form a super-directorate which would undertake to supplement the purely European aspects of NATO activity by mapping Western strategy in all other theaters. To back up his demands for this realignment of the Western position President de Gaulle has consistently refused to admit the primacy of United States interests in the alliance. The French fleet has been removed from NATO control and France has refused to permit the stationing of nuclear weapons controlled by U.S. forces on its soil; without a voice in the employment of nuclear weapons, which a directorate position would give him, de Gaulle holds that he cannot subject French sovereignty to the unilateral decisions of U.S. nuclear strategists. In adopting these tactics of pressure de Gaulle undoubtedly recognizes that he runs very little danger of alienating the United States—he is, in other words, fully aware that the geography of France makes her the heart of the alliance whether or not her cooperation is all that it should be. Hence, he continues to press for the adaptation of the alliance in such a way that France's position within it will be enhanced.

Another major aspect of the current French drive for national prestige and status in the international community is the ambitious nuclear weapons program, originally set in motion by Premier Mendès-France in 1954, and brought to first fruit in 1960 with the explosion of two plutonium fission devices in the Sahara Desert. These small test shots by no means made France a nuclear power, but they served, along with subsequent tests, notice that she is capable, even alone, of becoming one. It is clear that what the founders of the program hoped to accomplish by the tests—admission to the exclusive Western nuclear club with its perquisites of special prestige and access to U.S. production techniques as a means of speeding up national development of a full weapons system—has failed to materialize. The United States has taken the position that France does not yet qualify for receipt of still-secret, technical information, and is urging the French not to enter the devastatingly costly nuclear arms race. Partly because she has so far been refused admission to the club, however, and partly because of her anxiety to obtain a clear lead over any other European country (specifically Germany), which might also enter the race, France now appears more grimly determined than ever to proceed with the development and manufacture of nuclear weapons.

She is, furthermore, motivated by the desire to obtain the satisfactions of a nuclear power before a system of international controls or disarmament comes into force. With this in mind the French position on nuclear disarmament has remained steadfast for some years. She will agree to no disarmament proposals that envisage the elimination of nuclear weapons without the concurrent elimination of the means of delivery. Since it is in the area of perfecting missiles by which nuclear weapons are despatched to targets that France is farthest behind the other three nuclear powers, she is not likely to abandon her insistence on this equalizing factor in any future disarmament negotiations.

If France has not achieved all that she expected to in her nuclear weapons program to date, she has, at least, given considerable substance to her claim as a state with special powers, and with an unusual degree of technical development. Moreover, the large sums budgeted for extension of modern weapons research suggest that France will continue to use the distinction of being a nuclear power as a primary instrument of her foreign policy, regardless of the costs involved.

De Gaulle and West Germany

As early as 1944 General de Gaulle proposed to Winston Churchill, then Prime Minister of Great Britain, that their two countries should join in a close alliance which would rally the support of other nations seeking to prevent Europe from becoming a battlefield for the United States and Soviet Russia. This proposal was predicated on a permanently disarmed Germany, shorn of its capacity to upset the balance of the continent. In subsequent years, as the British cemented their special postwar relationship with the United States and as West Germany was rearmed by allied action, de Gaulle adapted his strategy, but did not fundamentally alter it. He now accepts the revival of West Germany as a *fait accompli,* and has apparently decided to put the strength of West Germany to the service of France and to use it as an integral element of his grand design for a European third force. To this end he has carefully cultivated his personal friendship with Chancellor Adenauer and has contributed mightily to the development of the Franco-German *détente,* which had, as we have seen, its origins in very practical economic considerations.

However, at the same time he has encouraged neither West German dreams of reunification with East Germany nor neutral disarmament zone proposals for Central Europe, which he feels would create a vacuum dangerous for France. He has indeed gone further and categorically declared that the question of Germany recovering the eastern provinces now part of Poland is a dead letter. Briefly the Gaullist conception of West Germany's role in European affairs appears to be that of a truncated, controlled, but effective state, developing a new and wholesome focus of loyalties, capable of acting in France's company independently of United States or British direction.

At times he has also hinted that such a Franco-German arrangement in Western Europe would in the future inevitably draw some of the Soviet satellites away from their close affinity with Moscow. Because his philosophy of international politics is drawn from a long historical perspective, he believes that the European quality of the Soviet satellites will ultimately triumph over their currently dominant Communist character. In like manner he has been known to muse publicly that Soviet Russia herself is more European than Oriental and will someday be driven back to Europe by the pressure of her bellicose Chinese colleagues. Whatever the validity of these arguments, they represent a potential disturbance for the United States. By merely threatening to make moves which would invite the Soviets to resume their European personality de Gaulle might one day obtain the initiative in Western diplomacy and strategy. His capacity for independent action has been amply proved in the past. Finally, the general's self-confidence, his penchant for broad international planning, and his infinite patience in the face of immediate realities are unique assets not always fully understood elsewhere in the West.

De Gaulle and Africa

The insistence on retaining a special interest in Africa which the other states of the world, at least of the West, must recognize and support constitutes a major drive in French foreign policy by no means original with de Gaulle's administration. It is first and foremost a projection of the more than a century-old colonial drive which won for France a huge empire in North and West Africa and Madagascar. The story of the evolution of this empire into independent states, and into the new independent nation members of the French Community, properly belongs in Chapter 10, but it should be noted here that, although the empire is largely dissolved, heavy French investments and thousands of French citizens remain in Africa, representing a stronger French presence than elsewhere in the old empire. Moreover, there is still hope in Paris that the new nation states of the old empire will retain their affection for France and that, even if formal ties become very thin indeed, a mutual interest in close cooperation between metropole and ex-colony will survive. The persistence of the war in Algeria, and the aggressive pan-African and pan-Islamic movements on the Dark Continent have seriously jeopardized the possibility of such fruitful long-range relationships' developing, but de Gaulle remains hopeful that these difficulties will be overcome in time.

It is the pressure for time to build new bridges to replace the old colonial ones that makes the French, and especially President de Gaulle, sensitive to criticism of France's policies in Africa and distrustful of other countries which presume to play a role there. The general once allegedly displayed his sensitivity on this score with a pungent anecdote: "If, Russia, America, or England reach the moon in a spaceship and are the first to plant their national emblem there, their feat will be described as an extraordinary scientific achievement. But if France sends a spaceship to the moon and plants its flag there, it will merely be cited as another example of French colonialism." There is much between the lines of this sardonic remark: the sense of frustration at not being granted Western support in Africa, at being refused the special recognition due a power with influence well beyond its own borders, and as always the wistful yearning for a seat in the company of the great powers.

Although de Gaulle has taken over an African foreign policy that was long in existence, rather than creating one of his own, he has linked it indissolubly with the other primary aspects of his foreign objectives. Thus France's independence, expressed in intransigence within NATO, is necessary for the preservation and perfection of her unique role in Africa. The demand for a place in the super-directorate of the West is also explainable on a similar basis: who is better qualified than France, with her intimate knowledge of Africa, to determine Western strategy in combating the spread of communism outside of Europe? Finally, de Gaulle's philosophy that nationhood is the fundamental fact of international life accounts for the peculiarly aggressive French attitude on Algeria. Settlement of the revolt is not simply a minor colonial preoccupation; it is essential to the survival of the Fifth Republic, and to perfection of a new image of France as a resolute and leading member of the Western World. For these reasons France expects forbearance from her allies in resolving the knotty Algerian problem. When forbearance is not forthcoming, or when French actions in North Africa are subject to criticism and debate in the United Nations, all other considerations take second place. She has kept the question off the agenda of the North Atlantic Council of NATO, and it is probably safe to say she would quit the United Nations rather than accept formal intervention by that body in the Algerian rebellion.

Conclusions

Any final view of French foreign policy leads to the conclusion that under the meticulous guidance of General de Gaulle its popular bases are in the process of being shifted. From a purely defensive expression of a national inferiority complex it is being redirected toward more positive, assertive goals. Thus de Gaulle no longer sees France as obliged to sit on the perimeter of the councils of the great powers. He assumes that France has a rightful place at the table; very often he arrogates to himself the leading role. When experience rebuffs, he does not hesitate to take an independent path by way of indicating that his country has a power and a policy of her own. And yet, as we indicated early in this chapter, there is dangerous fragility in all this. The game is being played by a great craftsman. If he should err—as for example in Algeria—or if he should be removed from the scene for one reason or another, the new tone of foreign policy, the assets of France, could be very rapidly destroyed. The revulsion in France to the prospect of another period of national humiliation or disillusionment could be very profound indeed, the consequences ranging from a possible brash striking out into international adventure of one sort or another, or a lapse into apathetic acceptance of France as a beautiful but faded backwater country nostalgically savoring her past.

10 - The French Community and Algeria

Introduction

For generations the French colonial empire provided U.S. movie producers with their most intriguing locales, the best of swashbuckling heroes, and the vilest of villains. Philatelists in every country coveted the colorful stamps which represented remote and exotic territories in virtually every corner of the globe. The French Empire was, indeed, greater than that of the British in size and second only to it in riches and diversity. To the French nation it meant first-class international status—at least as status was measured before World War II. It offered a wide network of military bases and an almost bottomless reservoir of recruits for the French Army; some of its land brought wealth to investors from metropolitan France or furnished colonists with comfortable incomes in settings that they rapidly converted into facsimiles of their homeland. At the same time the empire as a whole was a burden on the French treasury, and beginning in the late nineteenth century became more and more the focus of national political problems.

At first these problems were confined to the rivalry between competing colonial powers for influence in Africa and the Far

East. The visit of the German fleet to the port of Agadir in the French protectorate of Morocco intensified the tensions building between France and Germany prior to World War I. Great Britain played an ambiguous role in this affair because of her continuing antagonism toward France over conflicting territorial claims in Africa. During the interwar years new problems arose; the first of the native nationalist revolts occurred in the Rif country of Morocco and was finally subdued in old-fashioned colonial style after much bloodshed in the desert and political disenchantment at home. On the eve of World War II it was growing clear to many Frenchmen that the empire—or parts of it—constituted an expensive luxury, and that a reexamination of its ties with the motherland would be necessary when peace returned. By the time General de Gaulle undertook the slow reconquest of German-occupied France, the fundamental loyalty of the colonies to France became a crucial national question, because he was obliged to begin establishing the authority of his government-in-exile by consolidating his power and rallying support in the overseas territories. The difficulties which de Gaulle encountered at that time were mostly with unreliable French administrators, military officers, and settlers in the colonies who sympathized with the Vichy regime of Marshal Pétain.

After the war the problem of loyalties to France shifted levels. Whole native peoples either turned violently against France, or marched off into independence while retaining cordial relations of varying degrees. The successful rebellion of the Viet Minh in Indo-China cost France her principal holding in the Far East, debilitated and humiliated her armed forces, and gave birth to some of the ugly political discord in the metropole that culminated in the collapse of the Fourth Republic. The protectorates of Tunisia and Morocco won their independence with less bloodshed and bitterness, but in both cases France paid again a price in internal political distress. It is the continuing Algerian revolt, however, that has sapped France the most, and at this writing still threatens the very existence of democratic government, not only in the territory, but in Paris. Finally, most of the newly independent countries which formerly constituted the huge colonies comprising what was called French Black Africa and which have remained within a French sphere of influence, are being caught up in the cross-currents of the Algerian affair, and are under vigorous pressures to turn their backs completely on France. We return to a fuller discussion of the Algerian problem in the latter part of this chapter.

French Colonial Policy in Perspective

French empire building was achieved by and large in two dramatic bursts of exploration and colonization. The first in the seventeenth century was the more ambitious and saw the French flag planted in the New World as well as in India and the South Seas. In the territories acquired in this wave of imperialist expansion which have remained under French control—Guadeloupe, Martinique, Guiana, Réunion, and St. Pierre et Miquelon—there is a general disposition to accept an easy-going tutelage from France; the relationship between colony and administering power has had time to mature and solidify. In some cases the natives are as French as the most recently arrived official from Paris taking up his first overseas assignment. The first four are in fact overseas departments of metropolitan France, their inhabitants enjoy universal suffrage and elect deputies and senators to Parliament in Paris. St. Pierre et Miquelon, along with the other small and generally inconsequential possessions of France, are overseas territories with some degree of home rule permitted. However, for the most part the territories are administered from France, and legislation passed in Parliament in Paris does not necessarily apply to their inhabitants.

The second great wave of colonization took place in the nineteenth century, and it was in this period of expansion that France came into possession of its vast holdings in Algeria, Black Africa, and Indo-China, and established protectorates in Morocco, Tunisia, and the Levant. These were the territories that French leaders believed would make her great; they saw the influence of France spreading across the Mediterranean to encompass much of Africa and Araby. In Indo-China France hoped to counter or balance the preponderant influence of the British in India and Burma. But these also were the territories that would bring pain to France and that would finally make a mockery of the bright hopes of past generations. Colonial policy in the nineteenth and twentieth centuries was devised primarily with these larger and newer colonies in mind, and yet it has been, ironically, in the smaller, less important, and older colonies that the policy has worked to the satisfaction of the French—which is to say that the smaller territories have not chosen freedom as preferable to continued domination by France.

The basis of the colonial policy shaped by France in the late nineteenth and the first half of the twentieth century was, with some minor local variations, the theory of assimilation. On the face of it there was considerable merit in this idea. Plainly and simply stated it was that the culture of France, her way of life, her polity would be extended to the distant lands and bizarre peoples inhabiting them. France's *mission civilisatrice,* as this form of colonialism was called, would bear fruit as the native peoples became Frenchmen themselves and their countries either became parts of France proper or associated themselves with the motherland in some close-knit arrangement. Before World War II only a few native Africans and Indo-Chinese had in fact become citizens; most of these had become so by virtue of having served in the French Army. In Algeria administrators from the metropole found the durability of Moslem customs, institutions, and practices so formidable that it was found necessary to adjust to the importance of Koranic law. All sorts of experiments in blending French and Moslem ways of life were attempted to the confusion of the Moslems and the anger of the European settlers. On the other hand, many Africans, Indo-Chinese, and Arabs were educated in France and virtually converted into Frenchmen; impressive French-style universities and educational systems were set up overseas. Few opportunities, however, were offered the *élites* turned out by this educational system to plan and direct political systems of their own. Instead, if they were deemed trustworthy, they were put to work within the French administration as middle-level officials, where they soon became captives of the bureaucratic process. In the protectorates of Morocco, Tunisia, Syria, and Lebanon traditional local rulers clung doggedly to the shreds of sovereignty left to them by French governors-general. Even those who cooperated and collaborated most openly with their French tutors, in order to maintain their own special privileges and positions, contributed to the sense of nationalism that was slowly developing in their countries simply by continuing to symbolize an alternative to loyalty to France. In Indo-China corrupt and sometimes wickedly irresponsible native leaders kept control of the reins of power for decades by turning their native critics off against the French. In the long run the traditionalist leaders did not benefit from these tactics, but the Communist-led Viet Minh did.

Besides the basic fallacy in the assimilation policy—the assumption that all native peoples if offered the opportunity would want to become Frenchmen—three major weaknesses in the implementation of the policy eventually undermined it. First, in many instances wide gaps existed between theory and practice, between enunciation of the outlines of a colonial policy in Paris and its enforcement on the scene. Few settlers or colonial administrators living in the midst of what were for the most part backward peoples took comfort in the notion that their indigenous neighbors from the squalid native quarters or crowded *medinas* were potentially their equals, or even that the day of their maturity was near at hand. A strong tendency to thwart the meaning and purpose of colonial directives issued in Paris developed and was often abetted by the normally conservative military commanders posted to the colonies. The cumbersomeness of the French centralized administrative machinery facilitated the distortion and occasional defiance of directives from the capital by those responsible in the field. Thus, at best, the French populations of the colonies and the protectorates—especially in those areas where their numbers were large and investments significant—developed paternalistic attitudes; at worst, as in the case of Algeria, they absorbed the teachings of racists and religious bigots and provoked a resentful and smolderingly angry native reaction against the French presence, whatever its purpose as described in Parliament in Paris.

The second major weakness in the implementation of the assimilation policy was largely a function of the first. French colonial administrations often found it expedient to support and identify themselves with traditionalist native leaders in their overseas territories—an error shared by other imperial powers. This the French did primarily because at the moment of colonization these were the only leaders on the scene, but also because local chiefs and *caids* usually proved themselves more receptive to the immediate benefits available in accepting French favors and protection against rival interests than did the still struggling and barely articulate progressive forces. When in recent years the worm turned—often in outrage against centuries of despotic and obscurantist rule by local potentates—the French found themselves backing discredited leaders. This was the case in Indo-China and in Tunisia, where popular political revolts rapidly took on nationalistic and anti-French overtones.

Finally, the assimilation policy came too late to be effective, or perhaps more accurately it was applied at a too leisurely pace to keep step with the racing tempo of nationalism after World War II. The rapid evolution—or collapse—of French colonial policy since that time suggests the rate at which time was running out for France.

While the fighting in Europe still raged, General de Gaulle convened in 1944 a conference of colonial administrators at

Brazzaville in French Equatorial Africa to discuss the postwar future of the empire. Although no native nationals were on hand as delegates, the conference laid down surprisingly liberal principles hailed everywhere as great advances. Equal rights and privileges for all regardless of race or creed were ringingly proclaimed, the development of local administrations was promised, as well as entry to the highest ranks of French officialdom for the native born. In addition, steps were taken to set up an extensive investment institution in Paris for the development of the overseas territories. There was, significantly, no mention of training local leaders for responsibilities in ultimately independent states. In fact, the possibility that a goal of French colonial policy might be to prepare territories even for autonomous status within the empire was specifically excluded in the public declaration issued at the conclusion of the conference.

In keeping with the spirit of Brazzaville the new constitution of the Fourth Republic contained elaborate provisions whereby the old institutions of empire were converted into a French Union. The fundamental concept of the Union was to shelter the diverse elements, both ethnic and political, which were French, under one juridical umbrella, to provide a role for each element whether it were metropolitan France itself, an overseas territory (such as French West Africa), or an associated state, as the protectorates of Morocco, Tunisia, and the Indo-Chinese states came to be called. The territories were represented both in the National Assembly and in a new consultative body with advisory functions called the Assembly of the Union. The associated states were also to be represented in the latter body and, with the President of the Republic, were theoretically to direct the executive affairs of the Union in a High Council. However, since Morocco and Tunisia boycotted the Union from its inception, the High Council never really functioned.

In retrospect, the French Union was a worthy experiment that never lived up to its promise because the basic colonial issues which it was supposed to assist French government officials in resolving were being dramatically affected by events at its core: in Indo-China by violence and in Tunisia and Morocco by a determined resistance to French domination. Later, when the Algerian revolt broke out it was discovered that France held that this conflict was no concern of the Union, because Algeria, plus its Saharan hinterland, had been incorporated into France proper and divided into several *départments.* Thus, the Union found itself operating in an artificial atmosphere. Its members were expected to help elaborate the ways and means of developing interdependent relationships between France and her erstwhile colonies, while the conduct of France in those lands where her presence was no longer desired tarnished her image in the territories still only lightly touched by nationalism.

After the fall of Dien Bien Phu, the loss of Indo-China, and the beginning of the Algerian rebellion, the Socialist Premier, Guy Mollet, finally decided that colonial policy toward the bulk of the remaining territories in Black Africa must be drastically revised and reshaped to meet the pressures for national expression sweeping the Dark Continent. In 1956 the Minister of Overseas Territories in the Mollet cabinet, Gaston Defferre, produced and pushed through Parliament, despite loud rightist outcries, a new statute revamping the whole structure of Franco-African relationships. This was the *loi-cadre,* or enabling act, which provided the guiding philosophy for dependent areas until the establishment of the French Community under de Gaulle. The *loi-cadre* recognized that African demands for the creation of political institutions of their own choosing and for the direction of these institutions by elected Africans could no longer be postponed. In some ways this concept was the antithesis of that of the Brazzaville conference. Institutionalization of specifically African political entities implied recognition that non-French institutions were acceptable and permissible. Moreover, as outraged right-wing critics correctly pointed out, the grant of autonomous governments to the Africans would simply be the first step in a rapid march to independence. Nevertheless, the *loi-cadre* obtained a healthy majority in the Assembly. The territorial assemblies of Senegal, Soudan, Guinea, Ivory Coast, Mauritania, Upper Volta, Dahomey, and Niger in French West Africa, of Tchad, Ubangi-Shari, Moyen Congo, and Gabon in French Equatorial Africa, of Madagascar, and of the two League of Nations trust territories of Togo and the Cameroun were all given new authority and increased jurisdiction over domestic affairs. Furthermore each territory was authorized to set up a Government Council, elected by its territorial assembly. Each council was headed by a French official, but included a prime minister also elected from the Assembly. France retained control of foreign relations and defense, some aspects of justice, and higher education. French commissioners in the old colonial headquarters of Dakar (for West Africa) and Brazzaville (for Equatorial Africa) were also charged with assuring that the several territories in their areas created more or less similar institutions and methods of doing political business. Thus, several individual states were born out of what previously had been both literally and politically a jungle.

The Africans quickly established functioning regimes and began almost at once to extend the authority and appeal of their new political parties beyond their own borders with an eye to establishing larger African communities. Further movement for the amalgamation of distinct states into regional confederations produced only fleetingly successful results, however, as immature governments found it difficult to overcome natural and traditional rivalries. It was this new congeries of semi-autonomous states—some of which chose intensely nationalist premiers like Guinea's Sekou Touré, and some of which were already under the effective control of more conservative leaders who had served in the parliaments and ministries of France, such as Léopold Senghor in Senegal and Félix Houphouet-Boigny in the Ivory Coast—to which de Gaulle appealed for support in endorsing the last great experiment in the evolution of French colonialism, the French Community.

The French Community

For all practical purposes, the French Community was the shortest-lived institution of the new Fifth Republic. In name it still exists, but the purposes for which it was planned and devised no longer have meaning; those states which originally were to compose its membership have drifted off into independence. Paradoxically, however, the Community may have succeeded far better than any previous device of French colonialism, if success can be measured by the degree of good will toward France remaining in her former Black African territories and the broad influence she still maintains there.

The Community was a logical, but nevertheless bold, extension of the *loi-cadre* concept of enlarging the autonomy of French overseas territories. When de Gaulle came to power he was confronted with serious dilemmas. On the one hand, he personally viewed the Black African empire of France as a substantial evidence of French power and international prestige, as concrete evidence of his assertion of French grandeur. The nation's position in Africa was one of the elements of international power which enabled him to claim for France a special role in the council of great states. On the other hand, nationalist rumblings in the African territories were growing threateningly loud; there was danger that they would soon break away as most of the rest of the empire had done—and the Frenchman in the street appeared to care very little. The second dilemma confronting the general was that he had been brought to power by men dedicated to the retention of Algeria as a part of France at all costs. Many of his original supporters were insistent that any further loosening of colonial bonds in Black Africa would simply encourage the Algerian rebels to continued resistance. Yet it was also clear that the *loi-cadre* system would not long satisfy the Africans and that, if France wished to avoid fighting to hold the remnants of her empire, she would have to relax her grip and reduce to a minimum the role of the metropole. De Gaulle acted characteristically; he ignored the most clamorous of his right-wing supporters, and appointed the Ivory Coast leader, Félix Houphouet-Boigny, to assist Michel Debré in drafting those articles of the new constitution that would apply to France's overseas holdings. Both men were instructed to scrap the French Union and to revamp entirely the relationships between metropole and dependencies.

Before the final draft of this section of the constitution was completed, the general took off on a flying tour of the Black African territories, testing opinion as he went, clarifying his own thinking in the process, and at virtually every stop making more explicit the limits to which France would go in accommodating the nationalist ambitions of her colonial peoples. What ultimately emerged was a plan generously designed to encourage the African states to remain in the French orbit of influence, associated with and assisted by France, but not dominated by her. Moreover, each state was offered considerable flexibility of choice in the path it might follow immediately and in the future. First, there were the provisions of the new constitution detailing the contours of the new French Community as envisaged by Debré and Houphouet-Boigny. The Community provided for a common citizenship, and for the self-administration of its member states. By the terms of the constitution the Community as a whole—that is, France along with the other member states—was responsible for the determination of foreign policy, defense, currency, economic and financial policy, and the preservation of basic raw materials. The Community also undertook the supervision of justice, higher education, national transportation, and communications, unless one or more of these activities were removed from the competence of the Community by special agreement of the member states involved. The Community was also given wide latitude to transfer common policy obligations from the Community as a whole to individual members, or vice versa, a feature which gave substance to de Gaulle's promise that the African member states could develop fully autonomous regimes at their own tempo.

Not unnaturally the French Republic was given a primary position in the institutions of the Community. The president of France serves as president of the Community and, in the words of the constitution, "presides over the Community," and is represented in each of the member states. To emphasize the reciprocal character of the relationships involved, deputies of the national assemblies of the member states were given ballots in the presidential electoral college. The president heads an Executive Council of the Community which also includes the French premier, the heads of government of the member states and the French ministers charged with common Community affairs. The council was authorized to organize political and administrative cooperation between the member states, but in practice it listened to formal presentations of French policy by the president and on a more informal basis served as a convenient body for the negotiation of problems arising between France and the lesser members. The constitution also called for a Community Senate, charged with the discussion of financial and economic inter-relationships between the members as well as treaties involving Community obligations, and a Court of Arbitration to settle disputes between two or more African members. The Senate met but once and its deliberations were not significant. Some two-thirds of its members were elected from France proper—a fact that justifiably troubled the African members. The court was never convened nor even organized and there is little likelihood now that it ever will be.

As drawn, the Community was a flexible instrument, capable of adaptation to the evolving needs of the disparate peoples and states it was supposed to serve. However, in the interest of indicating the good faith of his oft-declared intention not to force any territory (other than Algeria) to remain with France unwillingly, General de Gaulle insisted that the overseas territories acknowledge their acceptance of membership in the Community or of some other status in advance of its going into effect. Thus, the territories were asked to express by referendum their choice of one of three options: (1) membership in the Community, (2) continuation as an overseas territory linked directly with France, and (3) outright secession—which, the general warned, would mean the immediate dissolution of all ties, financial, and moral, as well as political. In the balloting that followed only Guinea chose secession; the departure of French officials was rapid and bitter. The smaller territories, such as French Somaliland, the Comorro Archipelago, and a few others opted for direct attachment to France. Except for Guinea, all the other Black Africa states and Madagascar chose membership in the Community. The overseas departments, Algeria, and the trust territories were not, of course, included in the balloting, their status having been already defined within the constitution. In short order twelve African states had reordered their constitutions to conform to the requirements of Community status and had been admitted to membership.

The readiness of most Africans to accept the Community plan offered by France can be explained in a number of ways. First the leadership *élites* of most of the states involved were dominated by political moderates and had strong ties with France through education and often through career training in the French civil service. The strength and the monolithic character of the political machines which many of them headed in their territories were sufficient to produce a favorable vote for the Community referendum if they themselves were assured of its usefulness. Second, the great majority of responsible African leaders were persuaded by the arguments of Houphouet-Boigny that only through continued association with France could the territories be sure of receiving the funds necessary to carry out their advancement to full maturity as independent states. Since he had been the minister in de Gaulle's interim government responsible for the funneling of aid to the Dark Continent, it was presumed that he, better than anyone else, knew the frame of mind of policy-makers in Paris. Third, the flexibility of the new Community arrangements offered balm for everybody. Those states who feared that the Community was a ruse to Balkanize French Africa by breaking it up into small territories which could be manipulated by Paris were reassured by a constitutional article indicating (albeit somewhat ambiguously) that member states could change their status within the Community, or in other words join with one another in federations or confederations. Finally, for the nationalists who regarded any and all advances in colonial affairs merely as stepping stones to full liberty, an unequivocal guarantee of independence, if a member state wished it, was written into the constitution.

The Community in its original form survived only a little

longer than a year. At this writing it is in an ambiguous limbo. In 1960 all the African members exercised their privilege of declaring themselves independent nations, some with careful preparation and concern for the *amour propre* of France, some with unseemly haste, and others reluctantly, presumably out of fear of being left behind. The few months life of the Community was crowded with constitutional and administrative spadework in Paris as the various participants groped for a functioning apparatus. The president quickly asserted the full powers of his office and established himself as the moving force in the Community. In the process, and without alienating the African members, he subsumed powers and responsibilities not implicitly contained in the constitution, and broadened the scope of the powers of the chairman of the Executive Council. However, the real political battles were going on in distant African capitals. Efforts at confederation, federation, and even merger were tried, failed, and attempted again between several congeries of states. Discussion of the natural and sometimes unnatural associations of states that appeared to be emerging in the latter part of 1960 and the early days of 1961 does not belong in this volume. It is sufficient to observe here that the political turmoil unloosed in the African states of the Community, plus the continuing stimulants of the Algerian rebellion and the Congo fiasco, sharpened the currents of nationalism throughout the area. Moderate political machines were forced by the burgeoning growth of more radical oppositions to take up the cry for independence. Nonetheless, only one country, the former territory of the Soudan, rechristened Mali, tore itself sullenly from French apron strings.

What formal relationships between the new African nations and the French Community remain is a moot question. The so-called Entente States—Ivory Coast, Dahomey, Niger, and Haut Volta—indicated they would not rejoin the Community after obtaining independence; the position of the other Black African states is less clear. French economic aid continues as in the past alongside a bewildering set of new and separately negotiated bilateral agreements that were drawn up between France and several of the seceding states at the moment of independence. The impressive residue of good will, and mutual cooperation, as well as the unruffled continuation of numerous French business, religious, and cultural interests, suggests that there are still solid grounds for adapting the Community institutions to another set of requirements, possibly resulting one day in a loose and informal association of sovereign nations.

In retrospect, the record of French colonial history is one of brilliant aspirations either never completely fulfilled, or thwarted by the rush of events, by disagreements between Frenchmen in Paris and Frenchmen in the field, or by external circumstances over which France could have little control. Despite failures, the weight of French influence, especially in tropical Africa, has been important; the culture of France has been spread, if thinly, over vast sections of the world as the initiators of the *mission civilisatrice* hoped it would. Moreover, the final experiment—the Community—may in time prove a blessing to France. She has demonstrated that she would and could keep her word to former colonial peoples by granting them their freedom when requested. Thus, the image of France may well be strengthened even in those areas where she no longer maintains the slightest legal position. This, too, however, will depend on the resolution of the Algerian problem and the amelioration of the bitter anti-French feelings it has aroused throughout Africa.

The Algerian Problem

Throughout the pages of this book the problem of the Algerian war has kept cropping up, sometimes interrupting the exposition at hand, sometimes raised as a caveat putting in question what has gone before, but always as a sword of Damocles hanging over the head of the new republic. The war has divided the French bitterly among themselves, and in six years time it has developed into an agonizing international conflict which forces most states in the world to take positions on one side or another. France, however, continues to regard it as an internal problem, since to admit otherwise would be to suggest she needed help in resolving the matter. President de Gaulle has staked his personal prestige on finding a solution more or less satisfactory to all parties, but if he fails the disaster may not only be a personal one. Democratic government may disappear in France, North Africa may become a Communist outpost, or both could happen. At this writing the problem appears to be reaching a new, possibly conclusive crisis. Thus we can deliver no final judgments here, but will simply review the principal forces at work and suggest what seems to be the most likely outcome of present developments.

THE FORCES AT WORK. Almost all the major elements in French life have become involved in the Algerian problem, but in addition powerful outside groups either are directly affected by the war or are attempting to interpose themselves in the crisis. The principal forces are ranged either against the rebels or against French retention of power and influence in Algeria. But in addition there are subtler conflicts between and within groups. Some elements, for example, while favoring independence for Algeria, do not wish to see it come about under the present rebel leadership; others, although basically sympathetic to France and French interests, have little confidence in the effectiveness of the policies she is pursuing. It was in the tangled web of these differences and clashing interests that the Fourth Republic became ensnared and finally smothered. Similarly, the currents and cross-currents of antagonisms generated by these conflicts have weakened de Gaulle's regime, openly threatened its existence on two occasions, and thwarted the General's primary domestic objective of unifying the French public.

At first the protagonists were few and their aims precise. A handful of tough nationalist Moslems, unknown for the most part outside of their own towns, but clandestinely joined together, undertook in 1954 to raise the population of Algeria against the French administration. That administration had been in Algeria since 1830. In fact Algeria had been an overseas department almost since then (although some rudimentary and largely artificial organs of local self-government had been installed after World War II); 1,000,000 Frenchmen lived in the department, had invested billions of francs there, and had known no other home for generations. On one point there was no question when Ferhat Abbas and his companions began their wave of terror in Algiers, Oran, and Setif. On all sides there was unanimous agreement: France must suppress this revolt as she would any disturbance by revolutionaries anywhere in her homeland. The liberal Premier, Mendès-France, in office at the time, who had liquidated the Indo-Chinese war and had set Morocco on its road to independence, never hesitated. In his mind—as in the mind of most Frenchmen—Algeria was part of France. Large numbers of troops were quickly committed to the suppression of the rebels, but before long it became apparent that the revolt was not something that could be easily or rapidly rubbed out. The rebels soon grew skilled in guerrilla tactics and, when French military pressure became intense, withdrew to inaccessible retreats in the rugged Aurès or Kabylie mountains. It was the realization that the war might develop along the lines of the bitter, protracted, and ultimately frustrating Indo-Chinese revolution that produced among the French people second thoughts about the wisdom of pursuing it, divided the Moslem population of Algeria, and provoked the interest and alarm of France's allies, Algeria's neighbors, and the forces of international communism.

The Moslems

Arrayed against France is the *Front de Libération Nationale* (FLN), headed by a Provisional Government of the Algerian Republic (PGAR), with headquarters in Tunis, directed by a small steering committee composed of some of the original rebel leaders and a few younger ones who have proved themselves in battle or in diplomatic skill dealing with countries from which the rebels receive aid. The fighting arm of the rebellion is the *Armée de Libération Nationale* (ALN), which is controlled by a small War Committee of PGAR ministers. The PGAR has since its founding in 1959 developed many of the attributes of a government, but in essence it remains a revolutionary movement. It conducts the affairs of the rebel forces in Algeria, Tunisia, and Morocco and of the tens of thousands of Algerian civilian refugees in Tunisia and Morocco, directs networks of terrorists against the French both in Algeria and in metropolitan France, maintains relations with foreign governments, and actively lobbies in the corridors of the United Nations. Contact with the some half million Algerians living in metropolitan France is insured by PGAR-appointed chiefs of *Wilayas,* or geographical sections, into which the movement's covert organization is subdivided. *Wilaya* chiefs are responsible in their districts for the collection of funds to support the rebellion, for preserving the discripline of their followers, and for neutralizing—usually by violence or intimidation—fellow countrymen who are either noncooperative or who lean toward the small, moderate, rival nationalist movement of Messali Hadj.

In Algeria, itself, the influence of the FLN and the effectiveness of its control over the Moslem masses varies widely. The French insist that the rebel movement exerts its authority and influence only in those areas, usually the larger towns and cities, where rule by terror is possible. There is certainly some truth in this, as the long casualty lists of civilian Moslems, assassinated for suspicion of pro-French sympathies, give eloquent but somber testimony. Moreover, the FLN probably exercises a negative control on Moslem loyalties, the success of which is evident in such things as the reluctance of qualified Algerians to accept posts in the French administrative apparatus or their unwillingness to contest seats in municipal council elections. On balance, however, the situation is not as black and white as either the rebel movement or the French propagandists would like it to appear. Many Moslems have no love for either the French, especially the settlers in their midst, or for the FLN. For a number of years they played the game of concealing their hands, not wishing to make irrevocable commitments to either side, but bending when necessary to irresistible pressures from one or the other. They longed for a solution to the war although they cared little for the precise institutional form that would result for Algeria. In a vague sense they probably agreed on two other broad objectives: reduction of settler influence and domination, and the termination of FLN exactions and terrorism. The former challenged their dignity as human beings; the latter interrupted the routine of their meager and marginal existence. Most of them, however did not wish to become identified with the eventual loser in the bitter power struggle. These were the Moslems who welcomed de Gaulle's accession to power in 1958. In their eyes he seemed to be promising the best of all worlds: a determination to undercut the privileges and the arbitrary rule of the European settler class and an equally determined stand against abandoning the Moslem masses to the mercies of the hardened FLN leaders. As the war crisis continued, however, and an end to hostilities became increasingly more important to metropolitan Frenchmen than the shape of a final settlement, the Moslems in Algeria realistically began a reassessment of their relationships with the FLN.

The Settlers

As we have seen, the large European population of Algeria —which is as much Spanish and Italian in origin as it is French— considers Algeria to be its true home. Many, especially the large colony of Spanish civil war refugees, have no motherland to which they could return. Of the French, few are recent enough arrivals to have retained close ties with the towns or provinces in France from which their families emigrated. Almost all industry, the transportation and communication systems, much of trade and banking, are either owned and operated by European interests or by the French state. The French government, itself, has over the years built up an enormous infrastructure of schools, hospitals, roads, docks, bridges, and of course, the highly significant pipeline stations connecting the rich Saharan oil fields with Algerian ports. In short, to the extent that Algeria is a modern state it is a European creation. By and large the Moslems have been relegated to farming the poorer agricultural regions and to serving the enterprises of the Europeans. The pride of the Europeans in the economy, their vast agricultural holdings, and the culture they have established in the country is considerable.

The European insists that French Algeria was built from nothing, that before the conquest of a few scattered and primitive Arab communities along the coast in 1830 and the pacification of Berber tribesmen in the interior, no country, nation, nor even a unified people existed. Historically this is correct, but the European settler usually ignores the subsequent history of the Algerian Moslems. He fails to appreciate the effect of more than 100 years of European exclusiveness in the building of Algeria as an appendage of France, when only cooperative Moslems were admitted to positions of influence, permitted to amass land holdings of their own, or even given the opportunity for advanced education. He fails to mention the wage differentials between Moslem and European workers employed on the same job, the monopoly of hospital beds and schoolroom desks at the disposal of Europeans. He fails to mention the history of savage repressions of any nationalist demonstrations by the French Army, or the use of the *ratissage*—a systematized roundup and public beating of all male inhabitants—as a means of controlling unruly Moslem communities. It is true that some of these failings were beginning to be overcome in the years following World War II. Reforms were most often instituted at the initiative of the government in Paris, but sometimes also by the occasional liberal European leader who won control in an urban area, as in the case of Jacques Chevallier, former mayor of the city of Algiers.

By and large, however, the damage had been done by the prewar generations of settlers, and the legacy of Moslem-European distrust, animosity, and often fear and contempt, vitiated the impact of postwar reforms on the Moslem population. Finally, when Tunisia and Morocco seized their independence from France, the French Algerian settlers, sensing that nationalist agitation would soon erupt in their country of easy privilege and cheap labor, went on the defensive. In short they became more sensitive than ever to any moves to enlarge the liberties of the Moslems or to extend their political responsibilities.

The settler or *colon* establishment had strong political assets which it exploited skillfully in maintaining its privileged position over the rising pressure of the Moslems. Their assets included the deputies in the National Assembly representing the three overseas departments of Algeria, and close, sympathetic friends in the national administration and in the high command of the armed forces stationed in Algeria. The Algerian deputies were, almost to a man, conservative or reactionary spokesmen of large French enterprises in the territory, and they found willing support for their views from metropolitan right-wing deputies with heavy Algerian investments. In the 1950s the Algerian deputies as a group found themselves strategically located in the Chamber to lend their votes to Center governments, often dependent on rightist support for survival, in exchange for a go-slow policy on Algerian reforms.

A turning point in France's efforts to cope simultaneously with the rebellion and with the increasing hostility of the settlers against what they deemed to be Paris' flagging interest in continuing the war, came early in 1956 when the Socialist, Guy Mollet, took office as premier. He immediately flew to Algiers to install as Governor of Algeria the liberal military figure, General Catroux, who appeared to the *colons* as a symbol of appeasement. When the *colons* met the premier with a shower of rocks and rotten vegetables, he withdrew his candidate and instead named fellow Socialist Robert La Coste, a settler sympathizer himself, who appealed to the large French lower middle-class population of the Algerian cities. And so evaporated the first real opportunity to close out the Algerian war. Under La Coste's administration the electrified barrier which sealed off the rebels from their sanctuary in Tunisia was completed along the eastern boundary of Algeria. The future of Tunisia was from then on tied either to the complete success of the rebel movement or to the restraint of the French high command. As long as the latter was satisfied that the barrier kept only a minimum number of rebels from escaping into Tunisia, or from returning to Algeria after rest and training in the sanctuary, it might be expected to refrain from attacking across the border. Later Morocco was to fall into a similarly anomalous position—caught between conflicting desires to assist her Algerian brothers and to avoid recriminations or retaliation on the part of France.

In perspective, it is clear that the *colons* called the tune during the first four years of the Algerian war. Little was accomplished that ameliorated the situation, although some timid efforts were made by the severely inhibited Center governments of the Fourth Republic. Jacques Soustelle, former Governor General of Algeria, darling of the settlers, and a founder of the earliest Gaullists movement in 1947, became during these years a fearsome Assembly spokesman for *colon* interests and the policy of completely assimilating the Algerian territory with France. His forceful voice contributed heavily to the downfall of more than one of the last few governments of the Fourth Republic. In May 1958, when rioters in Algiers took over the central administrative headquarters of the territory in a gesture of defiance against the newly installed Premier Pflimlin who was suspected of being prepared to negotiate with the rebels, Soustelle fled Paris and insinuated himself into the command of the settlers' revolt. While the army insured the success of the coup, Soustelle's hasty trip to Algiers helped pave the way for de Gaulle's being called back to power after thirteen years in the political wilderness. Soustelle became a member of the general's cabinet during the interim period while the new constitution of the Fifth Republic was being written. He presided over the funeral of the Fourth Republic, but by remaining more faithful to the Algerian *colons* than to de Gaulle, he was soon excluded from power in the Fifth.

The Army

Because of the existence of the Algerian war, the French Army has held a dangerous margin of power in the Fifth Republic. It has thrown its weight into the determination of basic national policies, sometimes subtly, sometimes arrogantly, and many times with critical effect. In short, the army—important elements of which, notably the Psychological Warfare Branch, assisted in bringing de Gaulle to power—has been a major factor in the tangled dilemma of Algeria, and a force with which the president has had to reckon constantly in feeling his way toward a resolution. The army has insisted that its voice could not be ignored in the elaboration of policies for Algeria; it has always believed that it had a special stake in guaranteeing a military victory for France. The dedication of the French Army to this purpose obstructed progress toward a settlement, sharpened the divisions between Frenchmen and Moslems, and frustrated the efforts of political leaders to diminish the atmosphere of tension surrounding the whole Algerian question. More importantly, the power of the army grew so evident in the life of the nation that it became a major political force, which gave the impression that it held the life of the Fifth Republic in its hand.

The insinuation of the army into the forefront of French public life represented a rude turning in the nation's history. The military establishment has traditionally been regarded with suspicion by the average Frenchman, who, as we noted in an earlier chapter, is haunted by long memories of military threats to republican institutions and the political ambitions of antidemocratic generals. He remembers with misgivings the political legacies of the two Napoleons, the machinations of the Third Republic's first President, Marshal MacMahon, and the near success of another authoritarian romantic close to the turn of the century, General Boulanger. The sorry record of the Dreyfus affair, when individual rights were contemptuously flouted by a monarchist and antisemitic officer class, still lives vividly in the minds of most Frenchmen. Indeed, in no modern democratic country have military officers as a class been so distrusted by the society which it was their duty to protect. As a consequence professional military men in France grew apart from their fellow citizens, adopted an aloofness which in the eyes of the public made them even more suspect of harboring antidemocratic impulses and of secretly longing for the dissolution of civilian-dominated republican government. In reaction, the army, which literally sacrificed itself during World War I, outwardly assumed a posture of political neutralism, although its strength and its private political sympathies were so well known that it was dubbed, somewhat cynically, *la Grande Muette,* the Great Mute. By and large it did remain officially silent between the wars, although within the vast administrative apparatus of the state it operated as a conservative and often reactionary force, inhibiting by its very weight and prestige the freedom of action of governments, and obstructing or sabotaging the policies of progressive ministers. The army refrained, however, from involving itself openly in political and parliamentary quarrels.

Defeated quickly and ingloriously in World War II, the army fell to low estate. Its prestige was partially salvaged by the slashing return to France of de Gaulle's Free French Forces under the lead of such brilliant generals as Juin and de Lattre de Tassigny. However, the ultimate victory of France in 1945 was shared with the predominant forces of the United States and the Soviet Union. Moreover, credit for French success more often went to colonial troops, to *Résistance* heroes, or to amateurs who had won their spurs in the underground *Maquis,* than it did to the professionals. But it was the professionals who, even before the smoke had settled in Europe, were dispatched to Indo-China, to the protectorates of Morocco and Tunisia, and to garrisons in Algeria. In the decade following the defeat of the Axis powers, French officers—especially those of the army—rarely saw their French motherland and never once experienced victory. In far-away lands they were given hopeless assignments in the midst of hostile peoples. They often found themselves in command of Germans, Italians, and other mercenaries who fought not for France, but for money. Theirs was not only a solitary and unrewarding life, but a life that seemed somehow disconnected with France. At home the battles of the army went unnoticed except when reverses in the field necessitated higher military budgets or raised demands for "disengagement from colonial obligations."

It was the Indo-Chinese war that served as the forge on which the modern French military mind was shaped. This long, ugly, and desolate struggle embittered the combatants and drove the younger French officers who survived to search out new personal philosophies that would explain their relationship to France and a new military theory that would provide workable strategies for dealing with nationalist guerrilla wars and Communist penetration. Detention in Viet Minh prison camps or the agony and disgrace of encirclement and final surrender at the decisive battle of Dien Bien Phu were the experiences that motivated some of these officers to adopt what became known later in Algeria as the "mentality of the activists." Briefly, the activist reasons in this fashion: French postwar prestige and power overseas were frittered away because of political indifference in Paris where incompetent leaders squabbled over costs, hesitated to demand sacrifices of the public, and failed to secure the military cooperation of France's allies. At the same time the French General Staff tried to fight against native nationalist enemies with nineteenth century techniques. What was needed was the development of an all-embracing military philosophy which would blanket a whole people. In short, Communist-inspired nationalist leaders must be checked not only by the force of weapons, but by separating them from the people they would arouse, and by insulating the native peoples with a blanket of propaganda and an ideology that would enable them to resist nationalist blandishments.

The officers pursuing these lines of thought had clearly been affected by the writings of Mao Tse-tung pressed on them in Viet Minh prison camps, and some of them had at least flirted with the scrap ends of Nazi teachings mouthed by German officers in the French Foreign Legion. Colonel Roger Trinquier, who later became a central figure in defining political objectives for the army in Algeria and who for some years headed its psychological warfare bureau, wrote apropos the Indo-Chinese experience: "What we have to do is organize the [native] population from top to bottom. You may call me a Fascist, but we have to make the population docile and everyone's actions must be controlled."

When the scene shifted to Algeria and when French conscripts were committed *en masse* against rebel nationalists, these doctrines, which had only been evolving in Indo-China, began to receive wide circulation among the military. Eventually they were to contribute to a novel politico-military strategy for extinguishing the revolt. Basically it consisted of three elements: (1) Strangling the rebellion by cutting off the rebels' communications with their supply and diplomatic bases in Tunisia and with the urban centers in Algeria proper. (2) Sealing off the Moslem masses from nationalist infection. This was to be achieved both by regrouping whole Moslem population centers into areas controlled by the French, where rebel influence could be minimized, and by indoctrination. One positive means of enlisting Moslem support for the French cause was to recruit males into the French Army, thus engaging them to a point of no return, since they and their families immediately became prime targets of FLN terrorism. (3) Political action within France itself to obtain support for military objectives, for the army's mission of winning Moslem sympathies to its side, and above all for staking everything on the achievement of a victory for France. High-ranking officers, unaccustomed to participation in national politics, suddenly became openly aggressive; clumsy hints were dropped about the consequences for France's political future if the army in Algeria were forced by weakness or indecision at home to accept another, and final, humiliation in the field. To many professional military men, retention of Algeria as part of France became not only a prime political objective but a fundamental tenet of personal philosophy.

Nevertheless, the army has never been an entirely homogeneous force. Differences have existed between the so-called activist officers who are by and large found at the company and middle field grade level—captains, lieutenant colonels, colonels, and brigadiers—and the higher staff officers, many of whom owe their promotions to political ministers with independent views of their own on the Algerian problem. By no means the least significant of this latter group are those officers whose prestige was established while serving de Gaulle during World War II and who are completely loyal to the president. Moreover, in recent years there has been a steady influx of reservist officers to the regular service, who do not share the authoritarian and conservative traditions of their messmates. They are not persuaded by the arguments of the traditional careerists, whose families have served the French military for generations, that the armed forces are collectively the repository of national honor, and that when others (i.e., the politicians) would sell out the national heritage, they have an obligation to act, even if on the surface such action appears illegal. (Those who make this argument logically point to President de Gaulle as the living incarnation of this spirit.) Differences also exist between the officers who have served NATO and those who have been almost exclusively engaged in Algeria; the former tend to be concerned about the deterioration of NATO-committed materiel and manpower in the North African campaign, the latter bristle at the shallowness of an alliance which does not come positively to the aid of France in what they call the battle to save Algeria from communism.

Finally, differences developed within the armed forces, and between elements of the military and the settlers, over the basic Algerian policy which the leaders of the May 1958 coup devised in the exciting atmosphere of a military putsch. This was the policy of integration, the notion that only by fully integrating the political and administrative life of the territory with metropolitan France could Algeria be retained. If Algeria were indeed considered legally part of France, the national services (including the police and armed forces) would be perpetually committed to suppression of the revolt, and funds for the maintenance of a costly network of administrative controls and the expansion of interior communications would always be available from the national treasury. The integrationists also argued that placing Algeria completely within the political confines of the national government would enable 45,000,000 Frenchmen to outvote 9,000,000 Moslems on any conflict of interests arising between the two communities. (In Algeria alone, of course, Moslems outnumber Europeans 9–1.) To complete the picture, the settler integrationists quite inconsistently (but in their view, logically) insisted on special statutes for the Algerian departments of France whereby such national institutions as social security and wage controls would be determined on a different basis from those of the rest of France. The settlers argued that these arrangements were necessary to retain intact the cultural traditions of the Arab populations—in fact, they hoped by these devices to maintain white European advantages at the expense of the Moslems.

Thus, integration for the European settlers and metropolitan rightists was viewed as a means of bringing the full apparatus of the French state to the task of keeping the Moslems in a subservient position. The army, on the other hand, charged with the mission of creating positive Moslem loyalties to France, recognized that integration could only be undertaken if it promised effective elimination of social and economic differentials between Moslems and Europeans. To this end the French military establishment took the lead in the building of schools, training centers, public housing and other amenities for Moslems not welcomed by Algeria's European population. The army is proud of what it has done for the Moslems, and feels a special responsibility in assuring them that those who have cooperated with the French will not become victims of FLN revenge.

De Gaulle's Policies

If de Gaulle's acceptance by the French public in May 1958, following the *colon*-military putsch in Algeria, meant anything, it was that all were agreed he could somehow resolve the problem—either by winning the war once and for all, or by extracting France from the battle without a major loss of face. He picked up the responsibilities of leadership with no illusions about the complexity of the clashing interests involved. Essentially his policy has been to move toward a negotiated settlement with the rebels which would guarantee some minimal rights for resident Europeans and presumably refurbish cordial Franco-Algerian relations. For two years he acted with great caution and moved with what to his critics appeared to be unnecessary slowness and ambiguity toward these ends. To have gone faster, however, would have meant alienating the army completely; to have advertised his purposes clearly would have caused unrest within his own predominantly conservative UNR party. By inching forward slowly and obscuring his real intentions in clouds of puzzling rhetoric and formulae (e.g., "self-determination" and "an Algerian Algeria") he has kept those opposing any liberalization of Algerian policies off guard. On the most important occasions when the forces opposed to him balked openly—the settlers' revolt of January 1960 and the army mutiny of April 1961—his retribution was swift and harsh.

However, elements in France and elsewhere seeking a quicker solution of the war have charged that the president's hesitancy would drive the Algerian rebels into the Communist camp, poison French relations with Morocco and Tunisia, and eventually risk a military dictatorship in France. To a certain extent all these charges have been borne out. The rebels are increasingly dependent on Communist assistance; Morocco and Tunisia are suspicious; France itself is sickened by the use of torture in military prison camps, by drumhead justice for rebel terrorists, and by the increasing divisiveness within its own citizenry. Continuation of the war seems to many to be a hopeless outpouring of men and money and insures the isolation of France from its allies in NATO and its erstwhile friends in Black Africa. Yet none of these latter difficulties are irreversible—if a resolution is in fact obtained within a short time.

De Gaulle has shown that he is willing to go all the way in negotiating with the rebels. Most importantly, however, it also appears as this book goes to press that his chances of succeeding in this last delicate step are at least fair; that the tactic of confusing his opposition on the Right and ignoring his opposition on the Left may finally pay off. The crucial national referendum of January 1961 in which the voters of France and Algeria were asked to express their approval or disapproval of his Algerian policies to date and to sanction further steps toward setting up an autonomous Algerian republic, revealed three significant facts. First, despite the shrill objections of Soustelle's followers on the far Right that France was engaged in dealing off its birthright, and the charges of the Communists and the PSU on the Left that the referendum was a colonialist fraud, the returns in metropolitan France gave the president over 70 per cent of the vote cast and thereby virtually a free hand to settle the war in his own fashion. Opposition, such as it was, came pretty largely from those areas of the country—Corsica and other economically handicapped trouble spots—where the administration was held to blame, not for its Algerian policies, but for the existence of domestic hardships. Second, the massive abstentions of Moslem voters in Algeria, who were warned to stay away from the polls by the rebel government, demonstrated clearly how strong the influence of the rebels had become, as did the open demonstrations in favor of the FLN on the occasion of de Gaulle's Algerian trip a few weeks earlier. It exploded the myth of the European integrationists that at heart the Moslems wished to remain part of France, and equally punctured the army's claim that its policies of isolation and indoctrination were slowly winning over the minds of the Moslems. In no previous balloting in Algeria had abstentions run so heavily or had the FLN flag been so prominently displayed and joyously received.

Finally, the army's acquiescence in the holding of the referendum and its vigorous reaction to European extremists attempting atrocities on Moslems seemed to suggest that a certain fatalism had overtaken a good proportion of the French officers. Realizing that their claims to be winning the war militarily as well as psychologically were probably being frustrated not only by the will of their countrymen in France, but also by the stubborn fact that the Moslems, when permitted a free expression of their views, scorned France, many officers adopted a weary attitude of resignation in the face of the inevitable collapse of their cause. The ignominious collapse of the attempted putsch by General Challe and his associates a few months after the referendum emphasized what little real support the proponents of *Algérie Française* still enjoyed, even within the military itself.

Clearly the referendum was a mandate for President de Gaulle to continue his efforts to close out the war, but it also was a warning that this could probably only be accomplished through dealing directly with the rebel movement. Under the circumstances no other course seems feasible, and the general—who is as much a realist as he is a romantic—probably recognizes that although the referendum was a personal success for him, it also imposed limits on his choice of policies for terminating the war. If he should not act quickly to seek a negotiated solution with the rebels, his support at home would probably dwindle rapidly, the success of other national reforms would be jeopardized, and before long he might be confronted with an even more complex situation in North Africa as promises of Communist assistance to the rebel movement were made good. On the other hand, to agree to negotiate with the rebels would not guarantee a successful resolution of the war. There are many hard points that must be negotiated along the way, and many saboteurs lying in wait on the path. The question of European rights in a future Algerian republic, the relationship of the vast French Sahara to Algeria, and the future safety of the tens of thousands of Moslems now serving in the French Army or in the French administration are only a few of the issues which could cause negotiations to fail. Moreover, on both sides large numbers of discontented and disgruntled actors may be tempted to spoil the play at any time: right-wing French extremists and diehard activist officers, who have shown no reluctance to use violence to obtain their ends in the past; Moslem terrorists with scores to settle who may prove unresponsive to their commanders; and, finally, the vast number of simple bureaucrats, administrators, soldiers, and diplomats who may be involved in negotiating and implementing a settlement and who, consciously or unconsciously, may by their individual actions upset the delicate equilibrium of forces which today appears favorably balanced to the start of peace talks. If de Gaulle does, indeed, successfully maintain this precarious balance until a mutually satisfactory agreement is obtained, it will be his greatest triumph.

As for the Moslem Algerians, the future is cloudy at best. In the process of learning to live with the French for over 100 years and fighting them for at least seven years, they have developed a degree of national consciousness that never existed before. But their country is poor in many things, most notably in manpower skills. Moreover, the Algerian population is rising at one of the fastest rates in the world. By 1970 the Moslem population will have doubled itself in a decade. In the last analysis, the shape of the future appears to depend on the French. If a fruitful reciprocal relationship is worked out, at least some French technicians and some economic assistance may be available to keep Algeria afloat. If not, the radicals of the rebel leadership will almost surely dominate the country's political relationship, which means that they will root out French influence wherever it may be and probably be receptive to Soviet bloc sponsorship of their new nation.

11 - Problems of the Future

The highly tentative quality of this little volume reflects the somewhat cynical attitude of the French toward the Fifth Republic. Sceptical by nature, the Frenchman is dubious about the permanence of his new political institutions and is apprehensive about what he necessarily regards as the unpredictable course of political developments in the near future. Few public leaders and even fewer private citizens have openly espoused major changes in government structure, but changes are nevertheless anticipated. While no one can say when or how changes will come, there is general agreement that politics cannot long continue to be conducted in an atmosphere of national crisis, and that the government cannot rely indefinitely on the broad and unusual consensus which apparently supports de Gaulle as long as he keeps moving toward a solution of the Algerian war. Moreover, many Frenchmen have lived for some years with the fear that the army might at any moment take matters into its own hands and seize control of the government with disastrous consequences for France. Finally, in the more articulate circles a sense of urgency about the rush of events has developed: many fear that outside elements—the Communists, the allies of France, the United Nations—by intervening in Algeria might suddenly force drastic changes on the polity of France, and that President de Gaulle would be unhorsed and his "great experiment" discredited in the process. The future is obscure to all, frightening to many, and the general realization that things cannot remain as they are provides a frenetic background for the day-to-day operations of government.

Under these circumstances it is difficult to make confident judgments about the effectiveness and the vitality of the Fifth Republic. It may be appropriate, however, to speculate on the present course of the government and to offer some generalizations on the impact which the Gaullist experience is having on the French political consciousness. Any such discussion must consider both the possibility that the Algerian problem will be resolved in such a way that minimum damage is done to all the participants involved, as well as the grim prospect that de Gaulle will fail and that his regime will either deteriorate steadily or be brutally deposed. Because de Gaulle is, after all, mortal—despite the mystique surrounding his person—a brief examination of the viability of the institutions of the Fifth Republic without its linchpin must be attempted.

In its more than two years of life the Fifth Republic has plunged erratically through a number of crises that would have easily capsized any of its predecessors. Its leader has thereby earned a reputation for toughness, agility, and even political shrewdness. De Gaulle's survival was made possible, however, only at the cost of damage to his own public image and the erosion of traditional French sensitivities to deflation of democratic values. The president, who had a well developed sense of the style and technique of leadership when he took office, preferred to use his own personal talents to surmount political difficulties and overcome stubborn opposition to the regime, rather than to make the machinery of the new constitution more flexible and the workings of the new governmental institutions more palatable. At the same time he did not hesitate to recommend on short notice drastic constitutional changes as a means of legitimatizing a particular aspect of his policies. In some cases these personal tactics were necessary, as during the revolt of the settlers in January 1960, when the ugly mood of the Algiers mob, the army's initial reluctance to act against the insurgents, and the ill-concealed sympathy of some of de Gaulle's ministers for the insurrection threatened to throw France into political chaos. The revolt was abruptly ended when de Gaulle, appearing on the television screen in his World War II brigadier's uniform, sharply reminded the military officers of their duty—not to the republic, but to obedience to his orders. At that critical moment probably no other appeal would have succeeded. Again, after the mutiny in 1961 and the exposure of widespread sabotage within the administration and the military, ruthless use of personal powers under Article 16 to clean house was probably justified. In less chaotic circumstances, when the French African states began to demand and obtain their independence, swift constitutional adaptations of Community relations were generally agreed on as necessary to avoid giving the impression that France was obstructing African desires.

By and large, however, the president has chosen expediency before political diplomacy in the implementation of his plans, especially when the legislature has been involved. Because his official power is great and his public following so broad de Gaulle has felt free time and again to take the easy course of making major changes in governmental institutions, or in elaborating new policies by simply announcing his intentions, and requesting his advisers to discover legal justifications for his actions after his course was already determined. Moreover, he has brutally ignored Parliament. Following peasant riots in the winter of 1960, the required number of deputies petitioned de Gaulle to call a special session of the Assembly for the discussion of the government's agricultural policy. The president, whose minister of agriculture was already drafting new farm policies (most of which were later imposed by administrative fiat and were not the subject of legislation), refused to act on the petition, although the constitution seemed to suggest that he must convene the legislature on receipt of a legitimate petition. He coldly informed the deputies "that an extraordinary session would not be compatible with the regular functioning of the public powers." Although he thus avoided an embarrassing encounter with his political critics at a moment when the country was only just beginning to relax after snuffing out the settlers' revolt, de Gaulle in reality had nothing to fear from a legislative session on farm policies; his majority was safe and his staff was already completing first drafts of modest reforms. De Gaulle's explanation for his action satisfied few of the outraged deputies. He justified his refusal on the grounds that the legislators had bowed to the pressure of organized farm lobbies in petitioning for the special session, and inferred that he, as president, was duty bound to protect the institutions of the government from such debilitating practices. If the deputies were angered by his high-handedness, they scorned his paternalism and his condescension. He was fulfilling in their eyes the "papa" image mockingly evoked by the satirical *chansonniers* of the politically oriented Paris *caves*.

Much like a "papa" who, distressed by the incompetence and quarrelsomeness of his family, takes over the household routine and supervises all the individual actions of its members, de Gaulle has increasingly absorbed the responsibilities originally assigned his premier, the Council of Ministers, French ambassadors, and even on some occasions low-level bureaucrats. All matters of major government policy are determined and announced by him. Sometimes the Council of Ministers is informed a bare half hour before the general public of a new course the president is charting. Few appointments can be made without his agreement, and as we have seen in the previous chapter, his domination of new institutions, such as the Council of the Community, has been almost complete. The very office of the president has become a large and somewhat Byzantine affair. Each minister who deals with specific operational problems has a counterpart in the Elysée Palace whose counsel may have far more impact on the general than that of the minister. For every piece of legislation introduced in the Chamber of Deputies, there is an official Government view, drafted by an anonymous confidant of the president.

As more and more of the decision-making power is concentrated in the office of the presidency and wider and wider use is made of the Government's decree power, lesser officers tend to become increasingly timid and inhibited in exercising their own judgments. Action on public business, even of a most petty nature, awaits the opinion of the national "papa." Inevitably these conditions make for some blurring of lines of responsibility, for the misinterpretation of presidential directives, and for the intrigues of highly placed officials, who are confidently aware that de Gaulle cannot keep a personal watch on all governmental activities, and that his subordinates will usually be unwilling to root out potential saboteurs of government policy without first obtaining his agreement.

The public, too, is affected by the personality of de Gaulle and by his attempts to maximize personal control of public affairs. Confidence in the general, while still high, as the referendum early in 1961 indicated, is by no means as high as it was in the first year of his administration. Moreover, the institutions of the Fifth Republic excite neither respect nor interest, and secondary political figures are as much the subject of indifference, ridicule, or disdain as they were in the Fourth Republic. Because the political scene is so completely dominated by de Gaulle, the efforts of lesser leaders are frequently viewed as either superfluous, or if they presume to criticize the president's program, as obstructionist. The general's own behavior tends to reinforce these attitudes; he has, furthermore, done little to encourage the development of responsible political leadership that can serve the new institutions he has created when he departs the scene. Cabinet and undercabinet posts have remained remarkably stable and there are only infrequent opportunities for ministers to publicize their own endeavors; for legislative leaders the chances are rare indeed. Opposition leaders, of course, still do criticize the regime, as well as journalists and other public spokesmen. On some issues, such as the government's farm policies, the financial austerity program, wage controls, and the development of nuclear weapons, their criticisms have wide, and sometimes enthusiastic, followings, but under present circumstances they seem to have no sustained force.

The constant recurrence of public anxiety over developments in the Algerian situation, or the threats of right-wingers to topple the regime, inhibit the development of democratic political opposition against the one man whom the public seems to believe can and eventually will resolve the most immediate problems of France. Furthermore, the futility of systematic opposition in the face of the president's impressive parliamentary majority, of his tendency to act in disregard of the usual political restraints and niceties, and of his ultimate right to appeal for public support by referendum, already have discouraged many sincere and vigorous leaders who see no prospects of making their criticisms meaningful, and no alternative to de Gaulle's leadership. Thus Mollet, the Secretary General of the Socialists, one day offers motions of censure in the legislature which, if successful, might cause the dissolution of the Debré Government, and the next day publicly endorses the new Algerian policy of the president. Even the Communists, advised by their shepherds to vote "no" in the referendum of January 1961, apparently ignored orders and swelled the ranks of the affirmative voters.

The weakening of the "critical function" in French political life has emboldened the regime to operate ever more callously. Newspaper seizures for "public insults to the honor of the Army" were at one point so commonplace in Algeria that one of France's most respected independent newspapers, *Le Monde*, seriously considered restricting its circulation to the metropole. Even in France proper whole editions of some newspapers are from time to time confiscated "for reasons of State." The government-controlled broadcasting system unabashedly allots radio and television time to maximize its own position at the expense of oppositionist spokesmen. The use of torture in the French Army's Algerian prison camps is deplored in official government circles, but not halted. Instead, the full weight and majesty of the law has been thrown into prosecuting the author of an autobiographical account of life in a French prisoner-of-war camp. Reaction to these signs of decay in the political and social order of France comes, not unexpectedly, largely from intellectuals and students. The unions, conscious of de Gaulle's popularity and of the animosity between French-born and Algerian-born workers, are not as articulate in their protests. As we have seen, the leftist parties, with the exception of the Communists and the PSU, feel themselves trapped in a hopelessly compromised position, too weak to strike out effectively against the regime and uncertain whether, if they had the strength, this would be a wise move. While a solution to the Algerian problem is awaited, the alienation of French youth from its society and its public institutions continues. The spirit of protest against the excesses of state-contrived invasions of human liberty and individual dignity weakens. Concomitantly, the practices and habits of responsible political opposition to arrogant government fall into rusty disrepair.

Before these pages are printed, the Algerian problem may be terminated in one form or another, so we must look briefly beyond it. If what appears to be de Gaulle's firm resolve to give the territory its independence is thwarted, either by the overzealousness of the rebels, by wrathful, provocative action on the part of the European settlers and their military associates, or by the president's taking an inflexible negotiating position, not only will the pace of the war quicken and the undermining of what remains of the French love of democratic values continue, but de

Gaulle's failure may well become France's tragedy. In these circumstances rightist politicians, who have been bitterly opposed to de Gaulle's efforts to cut loose the Algerian albatross, can claim that their counsel has been right after all. Cries on the Left for the complete evacuation of Algeria by France will grow stronger, and the moderate voices of the democratic Center will be drowned out as the extremes assault one another verbally—and perhaps eventually physically. De Gaulle's vision of bringing the French people some measure of unity will be lost. His hopes of invigorating the concept of the grandeur of France will also be forfeited as the nation bitterly divides itself, sympathy for France in Black Africa evaporates, and her Western neighbors reassess the demands for status de Gaulle has made on them. In the face of these converging calamities neither the general nor the Fifth Republic in its present form would long survive.

On the other hand, a more or less graceful termination of the rebellion in Algeria which allowed the major participants some measure of face-saving, would not necessarily bring on the Golden Age in France. The antagonisms in French society already produced by the war and those existent long before it will undoubtedly be sharpened in the process of achieving a settlement. Over the long run, however, the damaged *amour propre* of bitter European settlers and disenchanted military officers can probably be assuaged. A more important aspect of the future will be the ability of the Gaullist regime to adapt to political conditions in which the hovering dangers of the Algerian emergency can no longer be invoked as justification for the authoritarian conduct of government business. The end of the Algerian war will remove the restraints that have been operating to withold the normal pressures on a French government. The demands of special interests, long muted so as not to jeopardize the delicate work of General de Gaulle, will be loudly put forward through the normal channels of political parties and pressure groups. The parties, themselves, will soon discover that their own members are no longer content to muffle criticisms both of the government and of their own leaders in the interest of maintaining domestic stability during a national crisis. For some, such as the Independents and the UNR, the cement which has artificially held them together in the face of adversity will weaken and fractionalization may occur. For others, especially the Socialists and the MRP, changes of leadership and orientation are likely as the rank and file forget the responsible roles played by their chiefs while the Algerian question was in the process of being adjudicated, and recall only that from 1958 onward the basic objectives and purposes of their parties have been submerged, overlooked, or weakened. In short there may be considerable flux in the life of the major parties. A likely result will be a revision of the coalition supporting the Government, whereby compensation for the decrease in conservative backing and the fragmentation of the Right is made by wooing the Socialists into participation. The latter, whose political life since World War II has been a series of compromises with party principle, may welcome offers of ministerial jobs and the opportunity to influence a primarily statist regime toward some form of national socialism.

Much will depend, of course, on the personal flexibility of de Gaulle or his successor. The development of changes in the party system, in the government coalition, and even in the character of political life requires a considerable reinvigoration of the primary institutions of politics, of which the most important are the representative bodies. At the moment there is no arena in which the force of one political ideology or method can be tested against another, or in which new political talents can be encouraged, matured, and ultimately given responsibilities. President de Gaulle has bypassed the legislature when possible; his Prime Minister, Debré, has described democracy negatively as "a process of pacifying political forces." In the perilous times through which his government has passed President de Gaulle has often identified opposition with subversion, and often he was correct. But this view, if it persists after peace returns to Algeria, can only turn the discontented and the democratic critics into the streets in organized displays of subversion. Hope is slim that the formidable ex-military strategist can in fact adjust to the conditions of peacetime politics. Once before, in 1946, he shrugged off the duties of provisional president of France in disgust at what he regarded as the selfish bickering of the parties and their leaders. No evidence suggests that he has changed his basic opinions on this score. Moreover, the few men he has brought along to be his most trusted ministers and personal representatives have been drawn largely from the ranks of the professional servants of the state, the civil service and the military. Without his personal backing they may well decide to return to their more familiar if less rewarding occupations.

Still, there remains the possibility that if the war ends to the credit of de Gaulle, he will assume a different political role than in the past and retreat from the center of the political stage. The premier would then become the focus of government activity, and without the constant protection of the president it is conceivable that the man and the office could over time become sensitive to the interplay of public and party interests, that the "critical function" in French public life could be refurbished, and that political energies would once more find constructive outlets in other than dutiful obedience to the chief of state. For this to take place a rethinking of the structure and theory of the Fifth Republic will probably be necessary. Today that regime rests on the unparalleled strength and powers of the presidency. The development of effective executive power has corrected a fundamental fault of both the Third and Fourth Republics. But the framers of the Fifth Republic's constitution and those who developed its political practices ignored the historical truth that government systems dependent on strong executive institutions either rapidly become authoritarian or else refract the executive power through effective, countervailing legislative bodies. Since in the Fifth Republic the legislature has been provided with no constitutional means to strengthen and make more fruitful its own complimentary power in the totality of governmental authority, it appears that such means will have to be developed for the legislature by action of the executive. The conventions and informal practices in the field of executive-legislative relationships that have grown up so far all have been in the opposite direction. They will have to be reversed by the positive action of either a president or premier who recognizes the necessity of political diplomacy, the smothering effects of consistent political paternalism, and the necessary stimulus to modern society to be found only in the educative effect of meaningful political debate.

Vital questions remain to be answered in France's immediate future. Are the institutions of the Fifth Republic viable for mid-twentieth century France? Can they meet the demands put upon them for the development of progressive social and economic policies that will compensate for decades of neglect and suffocating conservatism in these fields? Will they prove resistant to the selfish pressures of regional and vocational interests? Can they in time demonstrate sufficient effectiveness to reverse the traditionally distrustful attitudes of Frenchmen toward their government? We can in these closing lines only hesitantly point to the existence of certain factors in French society which may suggest the bases for answers to these questions. First, the capacity of the government to withstand particular pressures of entrenched and unprogressive business interests is probably better under the Fifth Republic than it was under the Fourth. The executive is less vulnerable to the special pleas and the highly skilled political blackmail of parliamentary spokesmen for these interests. Moreover, the Fifth Republic inherited a fortunate legacy that had been building in the final years of the Fourth—the rising power and influence of modern, expansion-minded business interests, encouraged to shake off the restrictive, over-protected economic philosophies of the past century by the crusading of such zealous technocrats as Jean Monnet and Pierre Mendès-France. But this in itself raises another specter in the minds of suspicious Frenchmen. Many fear that the technocrats will take over France and run it in the strait jacket of nationally devised plans, controls, and goals. And their fears are not unfounded. Among both the Gaullists and the Socialists there are formidable leaders who would mechanize the operations of society by reserving for the control apparatus of the state more and more of society's economic decisions and defining by fiat the scope of its social concerns. The leavening of technocratic expertise, necessary to any modern industrial society, with wise and humanistically attuned grass roots political counsel, is a challenge that the Fifth Republic must soon be prepared to face. Nothing in the institutions of the new republic need necessarily slow the momentum of the economy, or prevent the useful collaboration of pragmatic modernist planners and the representatives of the vast diversity of French provincial, vocational, and cultural life. In fact the strong executive could favor such fruitful progress, if it chose to develop the human talent which could sustain it.

Finally, to ask whether the Frenchman can ever be persuaded to accept fully such a government if de Gaulle is not at its helm, is in essence to ask whether the Frenchman can live comfortably with his past, or whether he will allow his past to dominate him. The greatest change that he has been required to swallow is the dilution of the role of the National Assembly. He has been asked to recognize, in other words, that the people of France do not constitute the sole repository of French sovereignty, but that it is also vested in the whole history and the culture of his society. These concepts are foreign to him; he reacts against them when they are verbalized, but in practice he has always been strongly nationalistic, and over the generations he has grown accustomed to the cumbrous permanent institutions of a centralized state, sharing power with the more transitory republican institutions. In short, it is possible that when the Frenchman becomes accommodated to the peacetime operation of the Fifth Republic, and especially if it can be adjusted to provide him some primary satisfactions, he may find that it is, after all, an acceptable arrangement of government institutions. A hopeful indicator of such conditions is the steady progress currently being made in France toward social leveling. The insistence on the primacy of the national legislature as a weapon against exploitation either by private interests or by an uncontrolled executive authority has been traditionally the watchword of the less fortunate classes and of their leftist parties. The gradual relaxation of social rigidities in the country—more the product of recent economic prosperity than of determined government action—has begun to diminish the impact of class consciousness and to reduce the political defensiveness of the industrial workers, peasants, and artisans. It is to these sectors of the population that the Fifth Republic must recommend itself positively in the years to come, if it is not to be neutralized by urgent pressures for a return to the more popularly responsive and the less stable institutions of the past.

The French Constitution*

Preamble

The French people hereby solemnly proclaims its attachment to the Rights of Man and the principles of national sovereignty as defined by the Declaration of 1789, reaffirmed and complemented by the Preamble of the Constitution of 1946.

By virtue of these principles and that of the free determination of peoples, the Republic hereby offers to the Overseas Territories that express the desire to adhere to them, new institutions based on the common ideal of liberty, equality and fraternity and conceived with a view to their democratic evolution.

ARTICLE 1. The Republic and the peoples of the Overseas Territories who, by an act of free determination, adopt the present Constitution thereby institute a Community.

The Community shall be based on the equality and the solidarity of the peoples composing it.

* Adopted by the Referendum of September 28, 1958 and Promulgated on October 4, 1958.

Title I–On Sovereignty

ARTICLE 2. France is a Republic, indivisible, secular, democratic and social. It shall ensure the equality of all citizens before the law, without distinction of origin, race or religion. It shall respect all beliefs.

The national emblem is the tricolor flag, blue, white and red.

The national anthem is the "Marseillaise."

The motto of the Republic is "Liberty, Equality, Fraternity."

Its principle is government of the people, by the people and for the people.

ARTICLE 3. National sovereignty belongs to the people, which shall exercise this sovereignty through its representatives and by means of referendums.

No section of the people, nor any individual, may attribute to themselves or himself the exercise thereof.

Suffrage may be direct or indirect under the conditions stipulated by the Constitution. It shall always be universal, equal and secret.

All French citizens of both sexes who have reached their majority and who enjoy civil and political rights may vote under the conditions to be determined by law.

ARTICLE 4. Political parties and groups shall be instrumental in the expression of the suffrage. They shall be formed freely and shall carry on their activities freely. They must respect the principles of national sovereignty and democracy.

Title II–The President of the Republic

ARTICLE 5. The President of the Republic shall see that the Constitution is respected. He shall ensure, by his arbitration, the regular functioning of the governmental authorities, as well as the continuance of the State.

He shall be the guarantor of national independence, of the integrity of the territory, and of respect for Community agreements and treaties.

ARTICLE 6. The President of the Republic shall be elected for seven years by an electoral college comprising the members of Parliament, of the General Councils and of the Assemblies of the Overseas Territories, as well as the elected representatives of the municipal councils.

These representatives shall be:

—the mayor for communes of fewer than 1,000 inhabitants;

—the mayor and the first deputy mayor for communes of from 1,000 to 2,000 inhabitants;

—the mayor, first deputy mayor and a municipal councillor chosen according to the order in which he appears on the council list for communes of from 2,001 to 2,500 inhabitants;

—the mayor and the first two deputy mayors for communes of from 2,501 to 3,000 inhabitants;

—the mayor, the first two deputy mayors and three municipal councillors chosen according to the order in which they appear on the council list for communes of from 3,001 to 6,000 inhabitants;

—the mayor, the first two deputy mayors and six municipal councillors chosen according to the order in which they appear on the council list for communes of from 6,001 to 9,000 inhabitants;

—all the municipal councillors for communes of more than 9,000 inhabitants;

—in addition, for communes of more than 30,000 inhabitants, delegates appointed by the municipal council in the ratio of one delegate for every 1,000 inhabitants above 30,000.

In the Overseas Territories of the Republic, the elected representatives of the councils of the administrative units shall also form part of the electoral college under the conditions to be determined by an organic law.

The participation of member States of the Community in the electoral college for the President of the Republic shall be determined by agreement between the Republic and the member States of the Community.

The procedures implementing the present article shall be determined by an organic law.

ARTICLE 7. The President of the Republic shall be elected by an absolute majority on the first ballot. If this is not obtained, the President of the Republic shall be elected on a second ballot by a relative majority.

The voting shall begin at the summons of the Government.

The election of the new President shall take place twenty days at the least and fifty days at the most before the expiration of the powers of the President in office.

In the event that the Presidency of the Republic has been vacated, for any cause whatsoever, or impeded in its functioning as officially noted by the Constitutional Council, to which the matter has been referred by the Government, and which shall rule by an absolute majority of its members, the functions of the President of the Republic, with the exception of those provided for by Articles 11 and 12 below, shall be temporarily exercised by the President of the Senate. In the case of a vacancy, or when the impediment is declared definitive by the Constitutional Council, the voting for the election of a new President shall take place, except in case of *force majeure* officially noted by the Constitutional Council, twenty days at the least and fifty days at the most after the beginning of the vacancy or the declaration of the definitive character of the impediment.

ARTICLE 8. The President of the Republic shall appoint the Premier. He shall terminate the functions of the Premier when the latter presents the resignation of the Government.

On the proposal of the Premier, he shall appoint the other members of the Government and shall terminate their functions.

ARTICLE 9. The President of the Republic shall preside over the Council of Ministers.

ARTICLE 10. The President of the Republic shall promulgate the laws within fifteen days following the transmission to the Government of the finally adopted law.

He may, before the expiration of this time limit, ask Parliament for a reconsideration of the law or of certain of its articles. This reconsideration may not be refused.

ARTICLE 11. The President of the Republic, on the proposal of the Government during [Parliamentary] sessions, or on joint motion of the two assemblies, published in the *Journal Officiel,* may submit to a referendum any bill dealing with the organization of the governmental authorities, entailing approval of a Community agreement, or providing for authorization to ratify a treaty that, without being contrary to the Constitution, might affect the functioning of [existing] institutions.

When the referendum decides in favor of the bill, the President of the Republic shall promulgate it within the time limit stipulated in the preceding article.

ARTICLE 12. The President of the Republic may, after consultation with the Premier and the Presidents of the assemblies, declare the dissolution of the National Assembly.

General elections shall take place twenty days at the least and forty days at the most after the dissolution.

The National Assembly shall convene by right on the second Thursday following its election. If this meeting takes place between the periods provided for ordinary sessions, a session shall, by right, be held for a fifteen-day period.

There may be no further dissolution within a year following these elections.

ARTICLE 13. The President of the Republic shall sign the ordinances and decrees decided upon in the Council of Ministers.

He shall make appointments to the civil and military posts of the State.

Councillors of State, the Grand Chancellor of the Legion of Honor, Ambassadors and envoys extraordinary, Master Councillors of the Audit Office, prefects, representatives of the Government in the Overseas Territories, general officers, rectors of academies [regional divisions of the public educational system] and directors of central administrations shall be appointed in meetings of the Council of Ministers.

An organic law shall determine the other posts to be filled in meetings of the Council of Ministers, as well as the conditions under which the power of the President of the Republic to make appointments to office may be delegated by him and exercised in his name.

ARTICLE 14. The President of the Republic shall accredit Ambassadors and envoys extraordinary to foreign powers; foreign Ambassadors and envoys extraordinary shall be accredited to him.

ARTICLE 15. The President of the Republic shall be commander of the armed forces. He shall preside over the higher councils and committees of national defense.

ARTICLE 16. When the institutions of the Republic, the independence of the nation, the integrity of its territory or the fulfillment of its international commitments are threatened in a grave and immediate manner and when the regular functioning of the constitutional governmental authorities is interrupted, the President of the Republic shall take the measures commanded by these circumstances, after official consultation with the Premier, the Presidents of the assemblies and the Constitutional Council.

He shall inform the nation of these measures in a message.

These measures must be prompted by the desire to ensure to the constitutional governmental authorities, in the shortest possible time, the means of fulfilling their assigned functions. The Constitutional Council shall be consulted with regard to such measures.

Parliament shall meet by right.

The National Assembly may not be dissolved during the exercise of emergency powers [by the President].

ARTICLE 17. The President of the Republic shall have the right of pardon.

ARTICLE 18. The President of the Republic shall communicate with the two assemblies of Parliament by means of messages, which he shall cause to be read, and which shall not be followed by any debate.

Between sessions, Parliament shall be convened especially for this purpose.

ARTICLE 19. The acts of the President of the Republic, other than those provided for under Articles 8 (first paragraph), 11, 12, 16, 18, 54, 56 and 61, shall be countersigned by the Premier and, should circumstances so require, by the appropriate ministers.

Title III–The Government

ARTICLE 20. The Government shall determine and direct the policy of the nation.

It shall have at its disposal the administration and the armed forces.

It shall be responsible to Parliament under the conditions and according to the procedures stipulated in Articles 49 and 50.

ARTICLE 21. The Premier shall direct the operation of the Government. He shall be responsible for national defense. He shall ensure the execution of the laws. Subject to the provisions of Article 13, he shall have regulatory powers and shall make appointments to civil and military posts.

He may delegate certain of his powers to the ministers.

He shall replace, should the occasion arise, the President of the Republic as chairman of the councils and committees provided for under Article 15.

He may, in exceptional instances, replace him as chairman of a meeting of the Council of Ministers by virtue of an explicit delegation and for a specific agenda.

ARTICLE 22. The acts of the Premier shall be countersigned, when circumstances so require, by the ministers responsible for their execution.

ARTICLE 23. The office of member of the Government shall be incompatible with the exercise of any Parliamentary mandate, with the holding of any office at the national level in business, professional or labor organizations, and with any public employment or professional activity.

An organic law shall determine the conditions under which the holders of such mandates, functions or employments shall be replaced.

The replacement of members of Parliament shall take place in accordance with the provisions of Article 25.

Title IV–The Parliament

ARTICLE 24. The Parliament shall comprise the National Assembly and the Senate.

The deputies to the National Assembly shall be elected by direct suffrage.

The Senate shall be elected by indirect suffrage. It shall ensure the representation of the territorial units of the Republic. Frenchmen living outside France shall be represented in the Senate.

ARTICLE 25. An organic law shall determine the term for which each assembly is elected, the number of its members, their emoluments, the conditions of eligibility and ineligibility and the offices incompatible with membership in the assemblies.

It shall likewise determine the conditions under which, in the case of a vacancy in either assembly, persons shall be elected to replace the deputy or senator whose seat has been vacated until the holding of new complete or partial elections to the assembly concerned.

ARTICLE 26. No member of Parliament may be prosecuted, sought, arrested, detained or tried as a result of the opinions or votes expressed by him in the exercise of his functions.

No member of Parliament may, during Parliamentary sessions, be prosecuted or arrested for criminal or minor offenses without the authorization of the assembly of which he is a member except in the case of *flagrante delicto.*

When Parliament is not in session, no member of Parliament may be arrested without the authorization of the Secretariat of the assembly of which he is a member, except in the case of *flagrante delicto,* of authorized prosecution or of final conviction.

The detention or prosecution of a member of Parliament shall be suspended if the assembly of which he is a member so demands.

ARTICLE 27. All binding instructions [upon members of Parliament] shall be null and void.

The right to vote of the members of Parliament shall be personal.

An organic law may, under exceptional circumstances, authorize the delegation of a vote. In this case, no member may be delegated more than one vote.

ARTICLE 28. Parliament shall convene, by right, in two ordinary sessions a year.

The first session shall begin on the first Tuesday of October and shall end on the third Friday of December.

The second session shall open on the last Tuesday of April; it may not last longer than three months.

ARTICLE 29. Parliament shall convene in extraordinary session at the request of the Premier, or of the majority of the members comprising the National Assembly, to consider a specific agenda.

When an extraordinary session is held at the request of the members of the National Assembly, the closure decree shall take effect as soon as the Parliament has exhausted the agenda for which it was called, and at the latest twelve days from the date of its meeting.

Only the Premier may ask for a new session before the end of the month following the closure decree.

ARTICLE 30. Apart from cases in which Parliament meets by right, extraordinary sessions shall be opened and closed by decree of the President of the Republic.

ARTICLE 31. The members of the Government shall have access to the two assemblies. They shall be heard when they so request.

They may call for the assistance of commissioners of the government.

ARTICLE 32. The President of the National Assembly shall be elected for the duration of the legislature. The President of the Senate shall be elected after each partial re-election [of the Senate].

ARTICLE 33. The meetings of the two assemblies shall be public. An *in extenso* report of the debates shall be published in the *Journal Officiel*.

Each assembly may sit in secret committee at the request of the Premier or of one tenth of its members.

Title V–On Relations between Parliament and the Government

ARTICLE 34. All laws shall be passed by Parliament.

Laws shall establish the regulations concerning:

—civil rights and the fundamental guarantees granted to the citizens for the exercise of their public liberties; the obligations imposed by the national defense upon the persons and property of citizens;

—nationality, status and legal capacity of persons, marriage contracts, inheritance and gifts;

—determination of crimes and misdemeanors as well as the penalties imposed therefore; criminal procedure; amnesty; the creation of new juridical systems and the status of magistrates;

—the basis, the rate and the methods of collecting taxes of all types; the issuance of currency.

Laws shall likewise determine the regulations concerning:

—the electoral system of the Parliamentary assemblies and the local assemblies;

—the establishment of categories of public institutions;

—the fundamental guarantees granted to civil and military personnel employed by the State.

—the nationalization of enterprises and the transfer of the property of enterprises from the public to the private sector.

Law shall determine the fundamental principles of:

—the general organization of national defense;

—the free administration of local communities, the extent of their jurisdiction and their resources;

—education;

—property rights, civil and commercial obligations;

—legislation pertaining to employment, unions and social security.

The financial laws shall determine the financial resources and obligations of the State under the conditions and with the reservations to be provided for by an organic law.

Laws pertaining to national planning shall determine the objectives of the economic and social action of the State.

The provisions of the present article may be developed in detail and amplified by an organic law.

ARTICLE 35. Parliament shall authorize the declaration of war.

ARTICLE 36. Martial law shall be decreed in a meeting of the Council of Ministers.

Its prorogation beyond twelve days may be authorized only by Parliament.

ARTICLE 37. Matters other than those that fall within the domain of law shall be of a regulatory character.

Legislative texts concerning these matters may be modified by decrees issued after consultation with the Council of State. Those legislative texts which may be passed after the present Constitution has become operative shall be modified by decree, only if the Constitutional Council has stated that they have a regulatory character as defined in the preceding paragraph.

ARTICLE 38. The Government may, in order to carry out its program, ask Parliament to authorize it, for a limited period, to take through ordinances measures that are normally within the domain of law.

The ordinances shall be enacted in meetings of the Council of

Ministers after consultation with the Council of State. They shall come into force upon their publication, but shall become null and void if the bill for their ratification is not submitted to Parliament before the date set by the enabling act.

At the expiration of the time limit referred to in the first paragraph of the present article, the ordinances may be modified only by law in those matters which are within the legislative domain.

ARTICLE 39. The Premier and the members of Parliament alike shall have the right to initiate legislation.

Government bills shall be discussed in the Council of Ministers after consultation with the Council of State and shall be filed with the Secretariat of one of the two assemblies. Finance bills shall be submitted first to the National Assembly.

ARTICLE 40. Bills and amendments introduced by members of Parliament shall not be considered when their adoption would have as a consequence either a diminution of public financial resources, or the creation or increase of public expenditures.

ARTICLE 41. If it appears in the course of the legislative procedure that a Parliamentary bill or an amendment is not within the domain of law or is contrary to a delegation [of authority] granted by virtue of Article 38, the Government may declare its inadmissibility.

In case of disagreement between the Government and the President of the assembly concerned, the Constitutional Council, upon the request of either party, shall rule within a time limit of eight days.

ARTICLE 42. The discussion of Government bills shall pertain, in the first assembly to which they have been referred, to the text presented by the Government.

An assembly, given a text passed by the other assembly, shall deliberate on the text that is transmitted to it.

ARTICLE 43. Government and Parliamentary bills shall, at the request of the Government or of the assembly concerned, be sent for study to committees especially designated for this purpose.

Government and Parliamentary bills for which such a request has not been made shall be sent to one of the permanent committees, the number of which shall be limited to six in each assembly.

ARTICLE 44. Members of Parliament and of the Government shall have the right of amendment.

After the opening of the debate, the Government may oppose the examination of any amendment which has not previously been submitted to committee.

If the Government so requests, the assembly concerned shall decide, by a single vote, on all or part of the text under discussion, retaining only the amendments proposed or accepted by the Government.

ARTICLE 45. Every Government or Parliamentary bill shall be examined successively in the two assemblies of Parliament with a view to the adoption of an identical text.

When, as a result of disagreement between the two assemblies, it has become impossible to adopt a Government or Parliamentary bill after two readings by each assembly, or, if the Government has declared the matter urgent, after a single reading by each of them, the Premier shall have the right to have a joint committee meet, composed of an equal number from both assemblies and instructed to offer for consideration a text on the matters still under discussion.

The text prepared by the joint committee may be submitted by the Government for approval of the two assemblies. No amendment shall be admissible except by agreement with the government.

If the joint committee fails to approve a common text, or if this text is not adopted under the conditions set forth in the preceding paragraph, the Government may, after a new reading by the National Assembly and by the Senate, ask the National Assembly to rule definitively. In this case, the National Assembly may reconsider either the text prepared by the joint committee or the last text adopted [by the National Assembly], modified, when circumstances so require, by one or several of the amendments adopted by the Senate.

ARTICLE 46. The laws that the Constitution characterizes as organic shall be passed and amended under the following conditions:

A Government or Parliamentary bill shall be submitted to the deliberation and to the vote of the first assembly to which it is submitted only at the expiration of a period of fifteen days following its introduction.

The procedure of Article 45 shall be applicable. Nevertheless, lacking an agreement between the two assemblies, the text may be adopted by the National Assembly on final reading only by an absolute majority of its members.

The organic laws relative to the Senate must be passed in the same manner by the two assemblies.

Organic laws may be promulgated only after a declaration by the Constitutional Council on their constitutionality.

ARTICLE 47. Parliament shall pass finance bills under the conditions to be stipulated by an organic law.

Should the National Assembly fail to reach a decision on first reading within a time limit of forty days after a bill has been filed, the Government shall refer it to the Senate, which must rule within a time limit of fifteen days. The procedure set forth in Article 45 shall then be followed.

Should Parliament fail to reach a decision within a time limit of seventy days, the provisions of the bill may be enforced by ordinance.

Should the finance bill establishing the resources and expenditures of a fiscal year not be filed in time for it to be promulgated before the beginning of that fiscal year, the Government shall immediately request Parliament for the authorization to collect the taxes and shall make available by decree the funds needed to meet the Government commitments already voted.

The time limits stipulated in the present article shall be suspended when Parliament is not in session.

The Audit Office shall assist Parliament and the Government in supervising the implementation of the finance laws.

ARTICLE 48. The discussion of the bills filed or agreed upon by the Government shall have priority on the agenda of the assemblies in the order set by the Government.

One meeting a week shall be reserved, by priority, for questions asked by members of Parliament and for answers by the Government.

ARTICLE 49. The Premier, after deliberation by the Council of Ministers, may pledge the responsibility of the Government to the National Assembly with regard to the program of the Government, or with regard to a declaration of general policy, as the case may be.

The National Assembly may question the responsibility of the Government by the vote of a motion of censure. Such a motion shall be admissible only if it is signed by at least one tenth of the members of the National Assembly. The vote may only take place forty-eight hours after the motion has been filed; the only votes counted shall be those favorable to the motion of censure, which may be adopted only by a majority of the members comprising the Assembly. Should the motion of censure be rejected, its signatories may not introduce another motion in the course of the same session, except in the case provided for in the paragraph below.

The Premier may, after deliberation by the Council of Ministers, pledge the Government's responsibility to the National Assembly on the vote of a text. In this case, the text shall be considered as adopted, unless a motion of censure, filed in the succeeding twenty-four hours, is voted under the conditions laid down in the previous paragraph.

The Premier shall be entitled to ask the Senate for approval of a general policy declaration.

ARTICLE 50. When the National Assembly adopts a motion of censure, or when it disapproves the program or a declaration of general policy of the Government, the Premier must submit the resignation of the Government to the President of the Republic.

ARTICLE 51. The closure of ordinary or extraordinary sessions shall by right be delayed, should the occasion arise, in order to permit the application of the provisions of Article 49.

Title VI–On Treaties and International Agreements

ARTICLE 52. The President of the Republic shall negotiate and ratify treaties.

He shall be informed of all negotiations leading to the conclusion of an international agreement not subject to ratification.

ARTICLE 53. Peace treaties, commercial treaties, treaties or agreements relative to international organization, those that imply a commitment for the finances of the State, those that modify provisions of a legislative nature, those relative to the status of persons, those that call for the cession, exchange or addition of territory may be ratified or approved only by a law.

They shall go into effect only after having been ratified or approved.

No cession, no exchange, no addition of territory shall be valid without the consent of the populations concerned.

ARTICLE 54. If the Constitutional Council, the matter having been referred to it by the President of the Republic, by the Premier, or by the President of one or the other assembly, shall declare that an international commitment contains a clause contrary to the Constitution, the authorization to ratify or approve this commitment may be given only after amendment of the Constitution.

ARTICLE 55. Treaties or agreements duly ratified or approved shall, upon their publication, have an authority superior to that of laws, subject, for each agreement or treaty, to its application by the other party.

Title VII–The Constitutional Council

ARTICLE 56. The Constitutional Council shall consist of nine members, whose term of office shall last nine years and shall not be renewable. One third of the membership of the Constitutional Council shall be renewed every three years. Three of its members shall be appointed by the President of the Republic, three by the President of the National Assembly, three by the President of the Senate.

In addition to the nine members provided for above, former Presidents of the Republic shall be members ex officio for life of the Constitutional Council.

The President shall be appointed by the President of the Republic. He shall have the deciding vote in case of a tie.

ARTICLE 57. The office of member of the Constitutional Council shall be incompatible with that of minister or member of Parliament. Other incompatibilities shall be determined by an organic law.

ARTICLE 58. The Constitutional Council shall ensure the regularity of the election of the President of the Republic.

It shall examine complaints and shall announce the results of the vote.

ARTICLE 59. The Constitutional Council shall rule, in the case of disagreement, on the regularity of the election of deputies and senators.

ARTICLE 60. The Constitutional Council shall ensure the regularity of referendum procedures and shall announce the results thereof.

ARTICLE 61. Organic laws, before their promulgation, and regulations of the Parliamentary assemblies, before they come into application, must be submitted to the Constitutional Council, which shall rule on their constitutionality.

To the same end, laws may be submitted to the Constitutional

Council, before their promulgation, by the President of the Republic, the Premier or the President of one or the other assembly.

In the cases provided for by the two preceding paragraphs, the Constitutional Council must make its ruling within a time limit of one month. Nevertheless, at the request of the Government, in case of emergency, this period shall be reduced to eight days.

In these same cases, referral to the Constitutional Council shall suspend the time limit for promulgation.

ARTICLE 62. A provision declared unconstitutional may not be promulgated or implemented.

The decisions of the Constitutional Council may not be appealed to any jurisdiction whatsoever. They must be recognized by the governmental authorities and by all administrative and juridical authorities.

ARTICLE 63. An organic law shall determine the rules of organization and functioning of the Constitutional Council, the procedure to be followed before it, and in particular the periods of time allowed for laying disputes before it.

Title VIII–On Judicial Authority

ARTICLE 64. The President of the Republic shall be the guarantor of the independence of the judicial authority.

He shall be assisted by the High Council of the Judiciary.

An organic law shall determine the status of magistrates.

Magistrates may not be removed from office.

ARTICLE 65. The High Council of the Judiciary shall be presided over by the President of the Republic. The Minister of Justice shall be its Vice President ex officio. He may preside in place of the President of the Republic.

The High Council shall, in addition, include nine members appointed by the President of the Republic in conformity with the conditions to be determined by an organic law.

The High Council of the Judiciary shall present nominations for judges of the Court of Cassation [Supreme Court of Appeal] and for First Presidents of Courts of Appeal. It shall give its opinion, under the conditions to be determined by an organic law, on proposals of the Minister of Justice relative to the nomination of the other judges. It shall be consulted on questions of pardon under conditions to be determined by an organic law.

The High Council of the Judiciary shall act as a disciplinary council for judges. In such cases, it shall be presided over by the First President of the Court of Cassation.

ARTICLE 66. No one may be arbitrarily detained.

The judicial authority, guardian of individual liberty, shall ensure respect for this principle under the conditions stipulated by law.

Title IX–The High Court of Justice

ARTICLE 67. A High Court of Justice shall be instituted.

It shall be composed of members [of Parliament] elected, in equal number, by the National Assembly and the Senate after each general or partial election to these assemblies. It shall elect its President from among its members.

An organic law shall determine the composition of the High Court, its rules, and also the procedure to be followed before it.

ARTICLE 68. The President of the Republic shall not be held accountable for actions performed in the exercise of his office except in the case of high treason. He may be indicted only by the two assemblies ruling by identical vote in open balloting and by an absolute majority of the members of said assemblies. He shall be tried by the High Court of Justice.

The members of the Government shall be criminally liable for actions performed in the exercise of their office and deemed to be crimes or misdemeanors at the time they were committed. The procedure defined above shall be applied to them, as well as to their accomplices, in case of a conspiracy against the security of the State. In the cases provided for by the present paragraph, the High Court shall be bound by the definition of crimes and misdemeanors, as well as by the determination of penalties, as they are established by the criminal laws in force when the acts are committed.

Title X–The Economic and Social Council

ARTICLE 69. The Economic and Social Council, whenever the Government calls upon it, shall give its opinion on the Government bills, ordinances and decrees, as well as on the Parliamentary bills submitted to it.

A member of the Economic and Social Council may be designated by the latter to present, before the Parliamentary assemblies, the opinion of the Council on the Government or Parliamentary bills that have been submitted to it.

ARTICLE 70. The Economic and Social Council may likewise be consulted by the Government on any problem of an economic or social character of interest to the Republic or to the Community. Any plan, or any bill dealing with a plan, of an economic or social character shall be submitted to it for its advice.

ARTICLE 71. The composition of the Economic and Social Council and its rules of procedure shall be determined by an organic law.

Title XI–On Territorial Units

ARTICLE 72. The territorial units of the Republic are the communes, the Departments, the Overseas Territories. Other territorial units may be created by law.

These units shall be free to govern themselves through elected councils and under the conditions stipulated by law.

In the departments and the territories, the Delegate of the Government shall be responsible for the national interests, for administrative supervision, and for seeing that the laws are respected.

ARTICLE 73. Measures of adjustment required by the particular situation of the Overseas Departments may be taken with regard to their legislative system and administrative organization.

ARTICLE 74. The Overseas Territories of the Republic shall have a special organization, which takes into account their own interests within the general interests of the Republic. This organization shall be defined and modified by law after consultation with the Territorial Assembly concerned.

ARTICLE 75. Citizens of the Republic who do not have ordinary civil status, the only status referred to in Article 34, may keep their personal status as long as they have not renounced it.

ARTICLE 76. The Overseas Territories may retain their status within the Republic.

If they express the desire to do so by a decision of their Territorial Assemblies taken within the time limit set in the first paragraph of Article 91, they shall become Overseas Departments of the Republic or member States of the Community, either in groups or as single units.

Title XII–On the Community

ARTICLE 77. In the Community instituted by the present Constitution, the States shall enjoy autonomy; they shall administer themselves and manage their own affairs democratically and freely.

There shall be only one citizenship in the Community.

All citizens shall be equal before the law, whatever their origin, their race and their religion. They shall have the same duties.

ARTICLE 78. The Community's jurisdiction shall extend over foreign policy, defense, currency, common economic and financial policy, as well as over policy on strategic raw materials.

It shall include, in addition, except in the case of specific agreements, the supervision of the tribunals, higher education, the general organization of external transportation and transportation within the Community, as well as of telecommunications.

Special agreements may create other common jurisdictions or regulate any transfer of jurisdiction from the Community to one of its members.

ARTICLE 79. The member States shall benefit from the provisions of Article 77 as soon as they have exercised the choice provided for in Article 76.

Until the measures required for implementation of the present title go into force, matters within the common jurisdiction shall be regulated by the Republic.

ARTICLE 80. The President of the Republic shall preside over and represent the Community.

The institutional organs of the Community shall be an Executive Council, a Senate and a Court of Arbitration.

ARTICLE 81. The member States of the Community shall participate in the election of the President according to the conditions stipulated in Article 6.

The President of the Republic, in his capacity as President of the Community, shall be represented in each State of the Community.

ARTICLE 82. The Executive Council of the Community shall be presided over by the President of the Community. It shall consist of the Premier of the Republic, the heads of Government of each of the member States of the Community, and the ministers responsible for the common affairs of the Community.

The Executive Council shall organize the cooperation of members of the Community at Government and administrative levels.

The organization and procedure of the Executive Council shall be determined by an organic law.

ARTICLE 83. The Senate of the Community shall be composed of delegates whom the Parliament of the Republic and the legislative assemblies of the other members of the Community shall choose from among their own membership. The number of delegates of each State shall be determined according to its population and the responsibilities it assumes in the Community.

The Senate of the Community shall hold two sessions a year, which shall be opened and closed by the President of the Community and may not last longer than one month each.

The Senate of the Community, when called upon by the President of the Community, shall deliberate on the common economic and financial policy before laws on these matters are voted upon by the Parliament of the Republic and, should circumstances so require, by the legislative assemblies of the other members of the Community.

The Senate of the Community shall examine the acts and treaties or international agreements, which are specified in Articles 35 and 53, and which commit the Community.

The Senate of the Community shall make executory decisions in the domains in which it has received delegation of power from the legislative assemblies of the members of the Community. These decisions shall be promulgated in the same form as the law in the territory of each of the States concerned.

An organic law shall determine the composition of the Senate and its rules of procedure.

ARTICLE 84. A Court of Arbitration of the Community shall rule on litigations occurring among members of the Community.

Its composition and its jurisdiction shall be determined by an organic law.

ARTICLE 85. By derogation from the procedure provided for in

Article 89, the provisions of the present title that concern the functioning of the common institutions shall be amendable by identical laws passed by the Parliament of the Republic and by the Senate of the Community.

ARTICLE 86. A change of status of a member State of the Community may be requested, either by the Republic, or by a resolution of the legislative assembly of the State concerned confirmed by a local referendum, the organization and supervision of which shall be ensured by the institutions of the Community. The procedures governing this change shall be determined by an agreement approved by the Parliament of the Republic and the legislative assembly concerned.

Under the same conditions, a member State of the Community may become independent. It shall thereby cease to belong to the Community.

ARTICLE 87. The special agreements made for the implementation of the present title shall be approved by the Parliament of the Republic and the legislative assembly concerned.

Title XIII–On Agreements of Association

ARTICLE 88. The Republic or the Community may make agreements with States that wish to associate themselves with the Community in order to develop their own civilizations.

Title XIV–On Amendment

ARTICLE 89. The initiative for amending the Constitution shall belong both to the President of the Republic on the proposal of the Premier and to the members of Parliament.

The Government or Parliamentary bill for amendment must be passed by the two assemblies in identical terms. The amendment shall become definitive after approval by a referendum.

Nevertheless, the proposed amendment shall not be submitted to a referendum when the President of the Republic decides to submit it to Parliament convened in Congress; in this case, the proposed amendment shall be approved only if it is accepted by a three-fifths majority of the votes cast. The Secretariat of the Congress shall be that of the National Assembly.

No amendment procedure may be undertaken or followed when the integrity of the territory is in jeopardy.

The republican form of government shall not be subject to amendment.

Amendments to the Constitution of October 4, 1958 *

ARTICLE 85. The provisions of the present title may also be amended by agreements concluded between all the States of the Community;

* Adopted by the French Parliament on May 18, 1960.

the new provisions shall be put into force under the conditions required by the Constitution of each State.

ARTICLE 86. A member State of the Community may also, by means of agreements, become independent without thereby ceasing to belong to the Community.

An independent State not a member of the Community may, by means of agreements, join the Community without ceasing to be independent.

The position of these States within the Community shall be determined by agreements concluded to this end, in particular the agreements mentioned in the preceding paragraphs as well as, should the occasion arise, the agreements provided for in the second paragraph of Article 85.

Suggestions for Further Reading

A wealth of books on almost every aspect of French political life exists for the interested reader. In addition, useful volumes specifically concerned with the Fifth Republic are now available, although most of the latter are general surveys of the whole apparatus of government and its political underpinnings rather than studies in depth. In this category the most ambitious and thoughtful—although among the earliest published—is Edgar S. Furniss, Jr.'s *France: Troubled Ally; de Gaulle's Heritage and Prospects,* New York, 1960. Of particular interest is Furniss' description and analysis of the deterioration of the Fourth Republic. Another, slimmer book of the same genre is the provocatively written *De Gaulle's Republic* by Philip M. Williams and Martin Harrison, London, 1960. A careful scrutiny of the new republic plus some useful documentary material is contained in the study by Roy C. Macridis and Bernard E. Brown, *The de Gaulle Republic—Quest for Unity,* Homewood, Ill., 1960. The keen British political scientist Dorothy Pickles is the author of a more modest volume devoted entirely to the de Gaulle government: *The Fifth French Republic,* New York, 1960. A sparkling book, which keenly analyzes the social changes that have overtaken France since the war and punctures many shibboleths about the persistence of traditional habits and values is *The New France* by Edward R. Tannenbaum, Chicago, 1961. Finally, it is hardly necessary to observe that a reading of de Gaulle's memoirs, preferably in the original French version, is essential to an understanding of what remains his republic.

Some perennially suggestive works which, although they predate the present government, provide a refreshing insight to French political traditions, ideologies, and the background of French politics are David Thomson's brilliant essay, *Democracy in France: The Third and Fourth Republics,* 3rd edition, London, 1958; Patrick E. Charvet's *France,* New York, 1953; the collection of short pieces contained in *Modern France,* edited by Edward M. Earle, Princeton, 1951; and the now classic critical commentary by the Swiss Herbert Luethy, *France Against Herself,* New York, 1955. The best short history of the Third Republic is Denis Brogan's witty and authoritative *France Under the Republic, 1870–1939,* New York, 1948; the best on the Fourth is Jacques Fauvet's *La Quatrième République,* Paris, 1959.

The only single-volume treatment of the present French constitution is Jean Chatelain's *La Nouvelle Constitution et la Régime Politique de la France,* Paris, 1959, a book which also contains helpful comparisons with earlier constitutions. Individual studies of the party system under the Fifth Republic are not yet available, but an excellent historical perspective on the subject can be had from François Goguel's *La Politique des Partis sous la Troisième République,* Paris, 1946, and Jacques Fauvet's *Les Forces Politiques en France,* Paris, 1951. French foreign policy in the period leading up to the establishment of the Fifth Republic is well explored in Furniss' *France: Troubled Ally,* and in John T. Marcus' *Neutralism and Nationalism in France,* New York, 1958.

Two standard works, although somewhat dated, are essential to a full appreciation of the French economy. These are Warren C. Baum's *The French Economy and the State,* Princeton, 1958, and Jean-Marcel Jeanneney's *Forces et Faiblesses de l'Economie Française,* Paris, 1956. On nationalized industry see Mario Einaudi, Maurice Bye, and Ernesto Rossi, *Nationalization in France and Italy,* Ithaca, 1955. The best analysis in the labor field is Val Lorwin's definitive work, *The French Labor Movement,* Cambridge, 1954. On business institutions see Henry W. Ehrmann's *Organized Business in France,* Princeton, 1957.

On the subject of local government a basic text is Bruce Chapman's *French Local Government,* London, 1953. For an inside, comfortable, and non-political view of French life in the small town see the delightful work by Laurence Wylie, *Village in the Vaucluse,* Cambridge, 1957. In a more business-like vein is the study by two sociologists, Charles Bettelheim and Suzanne Frère, of a small city: *Auxerre en 1950,* Paris, 1950.

No books in English have yet appeared on the French Community. A brief early study of an introductory nature is available in French: Gilles Néra's *La Communauté,* Paris, 1960. On Algeria more and more material is being published each month. The most useful are Richard and John Brace's *Ordeal in Algeria,* Princeton, 1960, and Germaine Tillion's *Algeria, the Realities,* New York, 1958. Sensational, but detailed and interesting, is the story of the Algerian coup that brought de Gaulle to power, by Merry and Serge Bromberger, *Les 13 Complots du 13 Mai,* Paris, 1959.

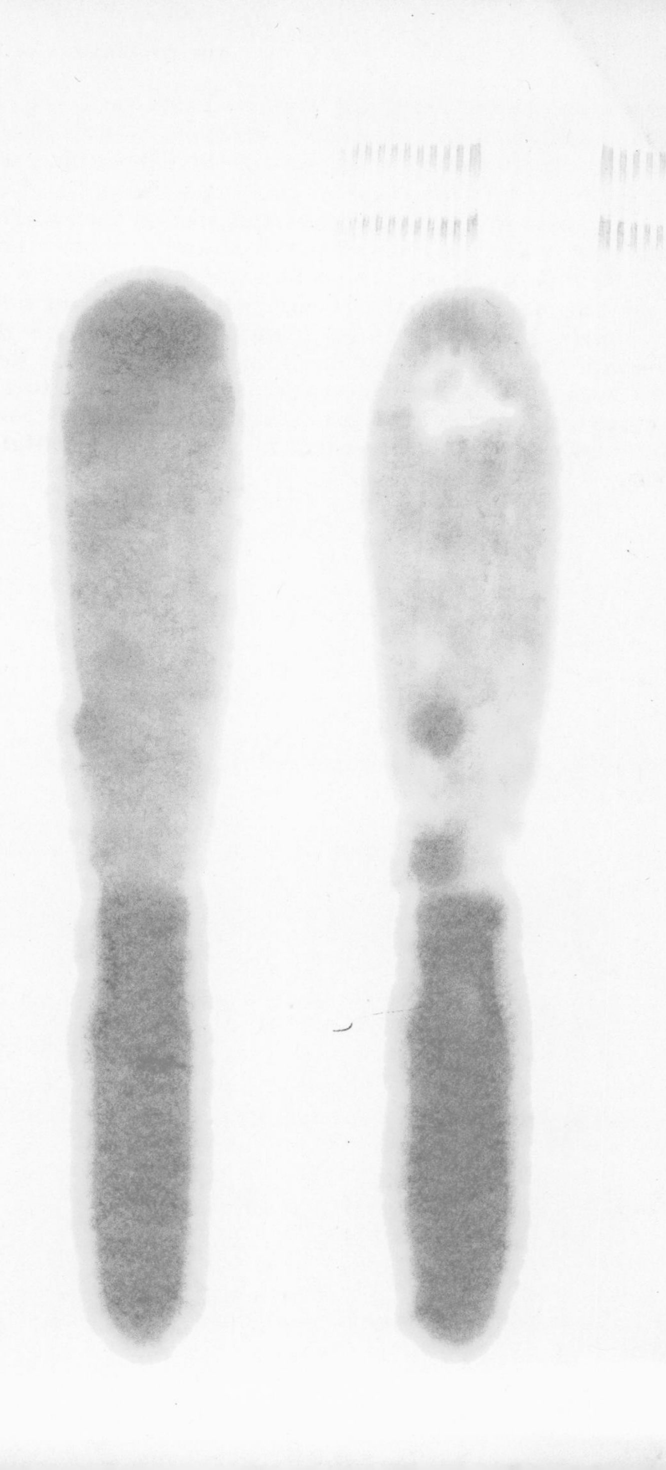

DATE DUE
